the GREAT ESCAPE

The GREAT ESCAPE

40 FAITH-BUILDING LESSONS
FROM HISTORY

CHRISTINE FARENHORST

Illustrated by Scott Wilkinson

P&R PUBLISHING

P.O. BOX 817 • PHILLIPSBURG • NEW JERSEY 08865-0817

Unless otherwise indicated, Scripture quotations are from The Holy Bible, New King James Version. Copyright © 1979, 1980, 1982, Thomas Nelson, Inc.

Scripture quotations marked (NIV) are from the HOLY BIBLE, NEW INTERNATIONAL VERSION®. NIV®. Copyright © 1973, 1978, 1984 by International Bible Society. Used by permission of Zondervan Publishing House. All rights reserved.

Page design by Tobias Design
Typesetting by Michelle Feaster

Printed in the United States of America

Library of Congress Cataloging-in-Publication Data

Farenhorst, Christine, 1948-
    The great escape : 40 faith-building lessons from history / Christine Farenhorst ; illustrated by Scott Wilkinson.
        p.   cm.
    Includes bibliographical references.
    Summary: Provides brief accounts of historical events, along with passages from Scripture and discussion questions, which introduce spiritual lessons.
    ISBN 0-87552-729-9 (pbk.)
    1. Devotional literature. [1. Prayer books and devotions.]
I. Wilkinson, Scott, ill. II. Title.

BV4832.3 .F37 2002
242'.62—dc21
                                        2001036936

To Nathan, Matthew, Emma, Ezra, Stephanie, Keturah, Marcus, and Judah,
and for all covenant children—young and old

Then Jesus called a little child to Him, set him in the midst of them, and said, "Assuredly, I say to you, unless you are converted and become as little children, you will by no means enter the kingdom of heaven." Matthew 18:2–3

Later On

My little one, at mother's knee,
I write this for a chosen child
To dwell on godly history
Where Hebrew ancients domiciled.
To let you always be aware
That witness clouds without compare
Surround your paths—encircle ways—
Greatly enhancing all your days
With faith—the surety of hope—
The covenant's kaleidoscope.

A silver lining and the first
Resplendent rainbow for a song,
A silver lining and a thirst
To laugh at Noah's beastly throng.
Ah, Pentateuch—inspired cry
Singing a Sarah lullaby
Of Isaacs, Jacobs and all such
That Laban men can never touch,
From Joseph and a dried-up well
To slavery of Israel.

Rameses building in a field
Of open sky and burning sun,

The warm and secret, reed-concealed,
Small basket of a child begun.
From plagues all ten and Red Sea moan,
To horse and rider overthrown,
Egyptians later could not see
The marvel of God's mystery
In taking for His very own
A Hebrew people, pilgrim prone.

It's in the wind and in the way
That Rahab's house did not fall down,
And in the fields where foxes stray
Burned up the produce of a town.
It's in the Moabitic smiles
Of Ruth who walked Naomi's miles.
It's in the guarding sentinel
Who saved the friends of Daniel.
Remember how they overcame,
By faith, by faith, by faith, their fame.

What shall I add, my little one,
To such a faithful multitude?
When all is said and all is done,
They urge your own similitude.
From Gideon and David tones,
Who conquered kingdoms with God's stones,
To Hannah's prayers and Mary's song
Shouting for joy, exultant, strong.
By faith to these be reconciled,
Do not forget to be a child.

Christine Farenhorst

Contents

Introduction

Although we live in an age of extensively complex communication systems—telephone, fax machines, e-mail—it cannot be denied that there is often a dearth of communication between parents and children. This can partly be attributed to the fact that many parents are caught up in a tremendously hectic lifestyle. Stay-at-home moms are not as common as they used to be and the frantic pace of life resulting in both parents working outside the home can have devastating results on family life. Tiredness, irritation through overwork, and the desire to get caught up with the ever-present housework can result in a maiming, or even a killing, of the ability to speak of God's power in day-by-day events. The media, with its grasping secularism, has become the main voice in many households as lax and laxer fathers and mothers relinquish their holds on the spiritual lives of their children.

The church of God is made up of many families and households. The church must be faithful collectively but also individually. Individual family members are to encourage each other. That is, they are to speak intimately to each other of the things pertaining to God's kingdom and of what He has brought about in their lives. If individual family members fail to speak to each other of these things, godly family life will disintegrate and become faithless.

Hebrews 3:12 tells us that we must see to it that there is a constant flow of uplifting conversation so that our brothers and sisters and children will have their sinful hearts pointed to their Savior. Verse 13 of the same chapter points out that we should encourage one another daily, before it is too late, so that we might not be hardened by sin's deceitfulness. Carelessness in not speaking of God's marvelous works; carelessness in failing to perceive the goodness with which He daily surrounds us; and carelessness in leaving manna, our manifold blessings of the Word, to spoil, can lead to a hardening of families' hearts. God forbid!

It is our prayer that these devotions may provide table or bed or wayside talk for many families—that they will encourage parents to speak with their children, and children to discuss with their parents what God's love and bounty has done in their lives and in the lives of past saints.

1

The Great Escape

Sometimes people do strange things—strange and dangerous things. Whether these people want to prove something, whether they want to do these things for attention, or whether they just have a sense of adventure, is not always known.

Harry Houdini was born in the latter half of the nineteenth century. Probably most people connect his name with that of a magician or an "escape artist." Harry (whose real name was actually Ehrich Wess), researched and studied many different types of locks and ways in which you could open them without using a key. He became so good at this that he had himself locked and chained inside a prison cell. Within eight minutes he was free and outside the prison door. People were impressed.

A few year later, Harry brainstormed a new escape trick. It was a little more difficult than escaping from a prison cell. As a matter of fact, it was seemingly impossible. With his wrists handcuffed, he plunged into an enormous milk can filled with water. The top of the can was then locked with six padlocks. In less than three minutes, Harry emerged from the can, wet but grinning. People were twice as impressed.

> *Therefore we must give the more earnest heed to the things we have heard, lest we drift away. For if the word spoken through angels proved steadfast, and every transgression and disobedience received a just reward, how shall we escape if we neglect so great a salvation, which at the first began to be spoken by the Lord, and was confirmed to us by those who heard Him, God also bearing witness both with signs and wonders, with various miracles, and gifts of the Holy Spirit, according to His own will? Hebrews 2:1–4*

Still not satisfied with his ability to amaze others, Harry went on to perfect a breathing technique through which he could live with an extremely small amount of air for almost two hours. It improved his water escape act and he felt no one could best him at it.

Harry Houdini died in 1926, as the result of a blow received on his abdomen. Although he had escaped from many and various kinds of cells and containers, he was not able to unlock the key of death.

Too bad Houdini didn't take Psalm 49:16–20 to heart. These verses say, "Do not be overawed when a man grows rich, when the splendor of his house increases; for he will take nothing with him when he dies, his splendor will not descend with him. Though while he lived he counted himself blessed—and men praise you when you prosper—he will join the generation of his fathers, who will never see the light of life. A man who has riches without understanding is like the beasts that perish" (NIV).

* * * * * * *

In 1968 a Mrs. Emma Smith was buried alive. She was thirty-eight years old and wanted to set a world record for staying under-

Although Houdini had escaped from many and various kinds of cells and containers, he was not able to escape from death.

ground. Mrs. Smith had three young children, enough to keep any mother alert and going. But somehow this woman from Nottinghamshire, England, felt an urge to do something unusual and strange—something that no one had ever done before.

A hole was dug into the ground. An eight-foot-long coffin, with Emma in it, was lowered down. One hundred tons of dirt covered both the coffin and Emma Smith.

The coffin Emma Smith was interred in was not an ordinary coffin. It was long enough so that Emma could move around. It had electric lights and heating. Also, from its buried position, a pipe ran to the surface providing food and drink. A closed-circuit TV allowed nurses to keep a constant watch to make sure the living "corpse" was all right. Emma even had a radio-telephone so that she could speak to her family. When she was bored, Emma wrote letters and knitted sweaters, and at night each one of her children could literally say, "my mommy's turning over in her grave." Perhaps, though, they would rather have had her tuck them in, have had her make their breakfasts, lunches, and suppers, and have had her there for any problems which come up day-by-day for children.

After 101 days in her remarkable coffin, Emma Smith was exhumed, or dug up. She climbed out of her box with a smile on her face. She felt she had accomplished something unique and was proud of that fact. Someday, however, she will be put back into a coffin, and at that time her eyes will be shut permanently.

* * * * * * *

There was another person who accomplished something no one else ever did. He entered the grave and conquered death. He entered the grave of His own free will. He did not do it to impress other people; He did not do it out of a sense of adventure. No, He did it because He loved His people and wanted to free them from the bonds of death. I guess you know that this person is Jesus Christ.

Those freed by Jesus from the bonds of death are one step up on Houdini and Mrs. Emma Smith. The greatest Escape Artist of all is their Savior and because of Him they are able to say, "God will redeem my soul from the power of the grave, for He shall receive me" (Ps. 49:15).

Food For Thought

1. Will the things that you do in this life, such as becoming a world famous doctor or an inventor or someone who earns a great deal of money, earn you a ticket to heaven? Why/not?
2. Is God impressed by your heart or by your deeds? Are the two connected? How?

2

Will Not Return To Me Void

A long time ago Egyptian farmers used to throw their seeds into the Nile when the water of that river was high. These seeds would embed into the fertile soil under the water along the shoreline. Then, when the water was low, they would harvest what had grown. The days between the seedtime and harvest were days of faith. The farmers could not really gauge the murky depths of the Nile to find out whether or not the seeds had taken root. They never knew how things were progressing. Yet time and again when it was the season for harvesting and the river was low, they would reap luxuriant crops.

Sometimes there are incidents and times in Christians' lives when they must live wholly in faith, not knowing whether or not a seed has taken root. There is a story of an old man who had four sons. He loved these sons exceedingly and brought them up as Christian children should be brought up. Each son, however, showed in his adult way of life that he had no desire to love God, and that he did not want to obey any of His commandments. The old man was a praying man, and he spent many hours each day praying for his children. Yet when it was time for him to die, not one of his children had shown any evidence of being converted. He was somber as he lay on his sickbed and had no words for his offspring. He did not smile and departed from this life in quiet reflection. As his four sons attended the funeral, they spoke with one another. "If indeed our father, who prayed much and was a godly man, should be so somber on his deathbed, how much more should we, who have lived godless lives, fear God," said the eldest. The others agreed with him. There was, consequently, a change in all their hearts and lives. It was the harvest of their father's prayers: a harvest he never saw, a harvest that had taken its time, and a harvest that was reaped in God's perfect time.

* * * * * * *

It generally takes a number of years before a child determines what it is that he or she would like to be, whether an accountant, policeman, housewife, or farmer. But sometimes, a desire is put into a person's heart, a calling, that is manifest even as a young child.

In the 1840s a young Welsh boy became convinced that Jesus' words at the end of Matthew 28 were specifically directed at him. He studied diligently at school and went on to seminary. During the course of these study years he was also given a sweetheart who shared his dreams of a mission field beyond Wales, beyond England. Financial support was garnered from the London Mission Society; prayers were offered; and China was the country to which the young man and his bride were being sent. The young man's name was Robert J. Thomas, and when he was ordained as pastor in a church in Hanover, Wales, it was the early summer of 1863.

Boarding a big ship, Mr. and Mrs. Thomas left their homeland in July of 1863. How they prayed together in their small cabin, thanking God for giving them opportunity to fulfill the Great Commission.

> *"For My thoughts are not your thoughts,*
> *Nor are your ways My ways," says the* LORD.
> *For as the heavens are higher than the earth,*
> *So are My ways higher than your ways,*
> *And My thoughts than your thoughts.*
>
> *For as the rain comes down, and the snow from heaven,*
> *And do not return there,*
> *But water the earth,*

How they praised His name for the comfort and support they had in one another because of common goals and understanding. They often stood at the rails of the ship's deck scanning the ocean for land, and when they first sighted Shanghai, they were very joyful that God had spared their lives from disease and drowning during the long and dangerous trip at sea.

Their joy was short-lived. Man plans but God decides. He always does. Shortly after landing, Robert's wife fell ill and died. He was now alone. He agonized over the question as to why his dear wife and helpmeet had died. Why had God brought her into China if only to take her so soon? Why had she been allowed to come so far? Why could he not have a partner in faith, one who would support him with love and compassion? In the end this sorrow, despite unanswered questions, brought him closer to God. He earnestly began working by himself for the Lord in China.

In 1866, having evangelized a few months in neighboring Korea, and having somehow mastered that language to some degree, Robert Thomas boarded an American ship, intending to travel further into Korea to spread the Gospel. The ship had been christened the *General Sherman* and took the route of the Taedong River. In

And make it bring forth and bud,
That it may give seed to the sower
And bread to the eater,
So shall My word be that goes forth from My mouth;
It shall not return to Me void,
But it shall accomplish what I please,
And it shall prosper in the thing for which I sent it.
Isaiah 55:8–11

some manner, perhaps because of its size, the *General Sherman* became grounded on a sandbar in the river. Seeing a big ship aground on their shore, Korean soldiers at that particular spot became afraid and suspicious. They were not used to foreigners, and they boarded the ship, heavily armed. The sun shone on the metal of their knives as they waved them about. They were unwilling to communicate and began killing both crew members and passengers at random. Robert Thomas realized that he would die also. He held out his Korean Bible to the soldiers, and his last two words were, "Jesus, Jesus." The Bible lay in a small pool of blood, and all the years of preparation in seminary and all the hours of prayer Robert Thomas had spent were apparently wasted. Three short years of mission work, and there was no clear harvest in sight.

But were those years really wasted? Was there truly no harvest? In 1891 some people came across a small guest house along the banks of the Taedong River in the area where the *General Sherman* had run aground. This house was unique in that it was wallpapered with paper of strange design—a design that had Korean characters/letters printed on it. The owner of the house explained that years ago he had torn the pages out of Robert Thomas's book and had pasted them onto the wall in order to preserve the writing. Many people came to stay in his guest house, and many people had read the walls, including himself. Thomas's life had not been in vain. God had used his death mightily.

Although there is much persecution of Christians in North Korea, the secret, or underground, church there was estimated to be at 60,000 people during the 1990s. The Word of God never returns to Him empty. It accomplishes what He desires and achieves the purpose for which He sends it.

Food For Thought

1. How is the Bible, the Word of God, a messenger?
2. If you read John 1:1,14, who actually is the Word of God?

3

John Gyles and Joseph

John Gyles ran like a deer—indeed, he ran like the wind—but he was not running fast enough. Pursued by an adult Indian brave, his short, ten-year-old legs were soon overtaken. Captured by those who had killed his father, young John saw his farm home in Pemaquid, Maine destroyed, and he watched as his mother, brothers, and sisters were tied together like cattle.

It was the young boy's last sight before he was carried north into what is now New Brunswick, Canada. It was 1689 and for the next nine years, as he grew up into a young man, he was a slave. At the beginning of his captivity, Gyles was often mistreated by the Indians. He knew both hunger and cold. But gradually, the natives grew tired of the too easy amusement of seeing him suffer. When the Indian who had captured John died, the tribe sold John to a French fur trader, Louis D'Amour.

Monsieur D'Amour bought the young lad out of pity and treated him kindly. John, in return, was a faithful servant, thankful for the good food and the clean clothing he once again had. He proved to have good judgment in trade and household affairs, and the family had respect for him. Often, however, John was tempted to run away. Was his mother

> *Therefore submit yourselves to every ordinance of man for the Lord's sake, whether to the king as supreme, or to governors, as to those who are sent by him for the punishment of evildoers and for the praise of those who do good. For this is the will of God, that by doing good you may put to silence the ignorance of foolish men—as free, yet not using liberty as a cloak for vice, but as bondservants of God. Honor all people. Love the brotherhood. Fear God. Honor the king. 1 Peter 2:13–17*

or any of his brothers and sisters still alive? But loyalty to the man who had saved his life, as well as faith in God, restrained him.

About a year after John was taken in by the D'Amour family, Louis had to leave on a long trip back to France. He placed the safety of his entire family and property into the hands of young John Gyles. He trusted the young man.

Several months after Louis's departure for France, word came that the English were planning raids on the French settlements in the area. John Gyles gathered this information with mixed feelings. He was English, after all, from Maine, and these raids might very well spell his freedom. But could he be disloyal to the master who had so trustingly placed his whole family in his hands? He prepared the family for flight away from the settlement, placing Madame D'Amour, the children, and provisions into canoes before pushing them off down river. Madame D'Amour had written a letter to the English commander begging him to save the settlement. As a last chore John fastened this letter to the gate. As he ran to the last canoe, to follow his mistress down the river, a man stepped out from behind some bushes at the river's edge. It was the English commander, doing reconnaissance before attacking. He spoke to John and John related his story. The commander presented John with an offer—a very tempting offer. "If," he said, "you help me find all the valuables hidden in this settlement, I shall help you obtain your freedom." How tempting this was for John Gyles. To have the help of higher authority in locating his family would be wonderful. It seemed to him the height of joy to breathe the air as a free man. But somehow John could not give way to his feelings. "I'm sorry, sir," he told the commander, "but I have promised to look after my master's family and property. I cannot help you."

The commander read the letter John had just posted on the settlement gate and decided against destroying it. But he seemed angry at John. "Have you no desire, boy, to see your mother again?" John replied that he thought his mother, who had raised him to live a life of gratitude and thankfulness to God, would not want him to spoil a trust. The commander then let John go, watching him as he got into his canoe to follow the family he served.

Three days later John stole back to the settlement with two other men and found it unharmed. Tacked behind Madame D'Amour's letter was another letter addressed to Monsieur D'Amour. It simply said that the settlement had been spared because of John Gyles's loyalty. The letter concluded with these words, "Send John Gyles to me under safe conduct before another month passes. I will see to it that he is restored to his mother at Pemaquid."

Recall the story of Joseph who trusted God and who was a slave in Potiphar's household. Joseph was faithful in all the tasks to which his master set him. We know that John Gyles, even as Joseph before him, put his trust in God, and we can conclude with joy that God rewards faithfulness. The tasks which God places in front of us may not always be to our liking, and human nature may often tell us to act in a different way than God requires of us. But the truth is that we must give service to whom service is due (as long as this does not conflict with God's law), knowing that we ultimately render *all* service to God.

Food For Thought

1. Read 1 Peter 2:13–17 again. Is there a Christian way to behave in any situation? Why/not?
2. When Peter wrote these words, the godless and cruel Nero was emperor. Did Peter mean that his fellow Christians should submit to Nero as the supreme authority? Why/not?

4

My Life For the Sheep

Crime, violence, and death—we read about these in the newspapers every day. We also read about them in our history books. It seems that every age casts evil shadows. Actually, we don't even have to go to newspapers and history books. Christian households also have squabbles and disagreements from time to time; Christian households can also harbor anger, hostility, and even hatred at times. It is a difficult thing for sinful man to overcome his natural desire to do evil; it is very hard for sinful man to do any good.

The author Charles Dickens wrote a book called *A Tale of Two Cities*. At the end of this novel one man sacrifices his life for a friend and says, "It is a far, far better thing that I do, than I have ever done; it is a far, far better rest that I go to, than I have ever known." *A Tale of Two Cities* is fiction set in the time of the Reign of Terror during the French Revolution (1789–1799).

There is a story recorded, not fiction but fact, which really took place during this Reign of Terror. It involved a father and son whose family name was Loizerolles. The son, a young man in his early twenties, had been brought before the Revolutionary Tri-

> *I am the good shepherd. The good shepherd gives His life for the sheep. But a hireling, he who is not the shepherd, one who does not own the sheep, sees the wolf coming and leaves the sheep and flees; and the wolf catches the sheep and scatters them. The hireling flees because he is a hireling and does not care about the sheep. I am the good shepherd; and I know My sheep, and am known by My own. As the Father knows Me, even so I know the Father; and I lay down My life for the sheep. John 10:11–15*

bunal (court) and was condemned to death for being an aristocrat. His father, an old man, white-haired and stooped over with age, refused to be separated from his son and accompanied him to prison.

The day of the young man's execution dawned. The father had spent every moment by his side, imprinting the son's face upon his heart and continually thinking and speaking of possible ways to escape. However, each thought was merely a castle in the air, and each hour merely brought the time of execution nearer. There was no mercy in the courts of the Reign of Terror. There was only fear and hatred, violence and anger. The young man, exhausted by nerves and idle hopes of freedom, fell into a deep sleep. The father, holding his son's hand, presumably for the last time, sat by his side.

While the young man was asleep, the jailer presented himself at the door of the cell with a squadron of soldiers. All the prisoners became tensely alert as the jailer read the names of those who were to come with him for execution without delay to the guillotine. When the name "Loizerolles" was read, there was no response—no one stepped forward. The young man was fast asleep. The old father, who had not had the heart to shake his son awake, was suddenly struck by a thought. And when the name "Loizerolles" was harshly called out for the second time, he gently loosened his grip on his son's hand and stood up in his place, joining the file of the condemned.

In low undertones the aged father then quickly gave a message for his son to those who remained behind in the prison cell. "When he awakes," the old man said, "I entreat you to calm him, and prevent any imprudent despair on his part from rendering my sacrifice useless. I have the right to be obeyed. Tell him that I forbid him to endanger the life which I have, a second time, given him."

The father then walked out, a stooped figure within the row of doomed men, to his death. Not too much later he lay his head on the scaffold and prayed, "Lord, watch over and protect my son."

Old Monsieur Loizerolles was a sinful man. Yet he was able to do some good. How was that possible? How could he? The Bible gives us the answer, clearly and simply. "Those who live in accordance with the Spirit have their minds set on what the Spirit desires" (Rom. 8:5b NIV).

Much more effective than sinful Monsieur Loizerolles's sacrifice was Jesus' sacrifice. Totally sinless, the Good Shepherd laid down His life for us, His children, His sheep (John 10:15).

We do not know how the son of Monsieur Loizerolles responded to his father's selfless act. Perhaps he committed foolish deeds and lived a life of wickedness after he came out of prison, thus rendering his father's sacrifice useless. Or perhaps he used the remaining years of his life to praise God in some way. We hope it was the latter. The wonderful thing about Jesus' sacrifice is that it cannot be rendered useless. That is because Jesus died for His sheep, and the Bible tells us that no one, no one at all, can snatch sheep out of God's hand (John 10:28–29).

The lives of the sheep are forever safe in the power of Jesus.

Food For Thought

1. The Heidelberg Catechism, Question and Answer 91, defines good works as works done out of true faith; works done in accordance with God's law; and works done to His glory. If Mr. Jones, who does not believe in God, donates some money to a charity, would this be a good work? Why/not? What did you do today that would conform to the Catechism's standard of "good works"?

2. Do our actions alone prove that we are one of Jesus' sheep? Why/not?

5

On Running a Race

On Sunday June 1, 1997, the Canadian runner Donovan Bailey and the American runner Michael Johnson ran a 150-meter race. The race was supposed to decide which of the two could run the fastest. The idea sprang from each runner's record time at the 1996 Olympic Games in Atlanta, Georgia. Bailey's time at the Games was 9.84 seconds in the 100 meters, and Johnson's time was 19.32 seconds in the 200 meters. Neither man had any admiration for the other. Bailey felt that he and his Canadian relay teammates had not been respected by American runners at the Olympics, and Johnson felt that Bailey had little respect for the Americans.

The Sunday, June 1, 1997, race was won by Donovan Bailey. Johnson was unable to finish running because of a pulled muscle in one of his legs. Bailey crowed with conceit after he won and made some very unkind and shameful comments about his opponent. Johnson and Bailey had been verbal enemies for a long time. They seemed to delight in taking every opportunity to say miserable things about one another, things that were repeated in newspapers, things that gave younger, would-be athletes a very poor idea of honest and fair sportsmanship.

> *I have fought the good fight, I have finished the race, I have kept the faith. Finally, there is laid up for me the crown of righteousness, which the Lord, the righteous Judge, will give to me on that Day, and not to me only but also to all who have loved His appearing. 2 Timothy 4:7–8*

Donovan Bailey earned $1.5 million for 14.99 seconds of running. This works out to about $100,000 per second.

* * * * * * *

The Olympic Games began in 176 B.C. in Olympia, Greece. They were held every four years but were disbanded by the Roman Emperor Theodosius (346–395) toward the end of his rule. Fifteen hundred years passed before they reappeared in Athens. The year was 1896. A Frenchman by the name of Pierre de Courbetin introduced the Games once more because he felt that competition with principles of fairness and honesty were good. From then on, with the exception of the time period involving the two World Wars, the Olympics were once again held every four years. (An Olympiad is a period of four years.)

Not all the Games had competitors like Donovan Bailey and Michael Johnson. In 1924, Eric Liddell, a very gifted twenty-two-year-old runner from Scotland was scheduled to run the 100-meter race in the Olympics. He was an excellent 100-meter runner and had been chosen to take a place on the British team in Paris. When the timetable of Olympic events was posted and the athletes gathered around to read when they would be competing, everyone was amazed to hear Eric Liddell announce in a quiet voice that he would not be running. The date on which he was posted to run was a Sunday—the Lord's day.

Eric Liddell's goal had been to run, not for Olympic medals that would fade over time, but for "an imperishable crown" (1 Cor. 9:25).

There were not many people who understood why Eric would not run on Sunday. Most people ridiculed him. They insisted that Eric could dedicate the race to God that Sunday. They also said that he was letting Scotland down by not running and that he was a traitor to his country. Eric was hurt by the various unkind comments, but he did not waver in his conviction that God's command to honor the Sunday would be obeyed by himself and that he was right in refusing to run on the Lord's day.

Because he was part of their team, the British authorities requested that Eric run in the 200-meter and 400-meter race in the Olympics instead of in the 100-meter race. They did not expect him to do very well, let alone win. After all, he was a 100-meter runner and that was the race, they said, where he could have expected to win a gold medal.

Against all expectations, Eric won a bronze medal in the 200-meter. A few days later when the 400-meter day dawned, there was not much hope for a gold medal for the British team. Right from the start, however, from the very time when the pistol went off, Eric leapt into the lead. Breathlessly, people watched him run. No one expected him to keep up his incredible pace. A 100-meter runner would soon tire and be overtaken. But as the other athletes began to bridge the gap, Eric, against all expectations, picked up more speed—and kept it up—until he reached the tape a full five meters ahead of everyone else.

Eric Liddell set a new world record that day: the 400 meters in 47.6 seconds. Suddenly everyone forgot all the bad things they had said about him; suddenly Eric was a hero. Eric himself was physically and emotionally drained. He was happy that he had won the much-coveted gold medal for his country. But he was also deeply grateful to God for allowing him to win. Prior to the race, Eric's trainer had given him a piece of paper, folded over so that he could not read it. Eric had thanked him for it and had not unfolded it until moments before beginning his run. In bold letters the trainer had written down, "In the old book it says, 'He that honors Me I will honor.' Wishing you the best success always." The words had encouraged Eric at the onset of the race, and now that the race was over, Eric knew that God had indeed honored his stand about Sunday running. The knowledge strengthened his faith.

Eric Liddell's goal had been to run, not for Olympic medals that would fade over time, but for "an imperishable crown" (1 Cor. 9:25). His later life testified to that. Upon completing his studies, he entered the Chinese mission field, laboring there until 1945 when, at the end of the Second World War, he died in a Japanese prison camp.

Many men and women in the past have boasted about their accomplishments in sports, even as Donovan Bailey boasted that he was the fastest man on earth. What these people fail to realize is that the only race in which winning really counts is the one in which the Lord, the righteous Judge, will award the crown of righteousness to all those who have longed for His appearing (2 Tim. 4:8).

Food For Thought

1. To be successful in running a race, to be successful in any sport, hard work and practice are very important. If you do not practice, you will not do well, let alone win. How can you practice for the race we all run toward heaven—for the battle we all partake in for Christ?

2. Did you ever refuse to do something on Sunday for the same reason that Eric Liddell refused to run? What was it?

6

The Source of All Beauty

She was not that old, barely a teenager, but her parents left her in charge of both the house and her two younger brothers while they went visiting. Perhaps this would not be so unusual were it not that the times were dangerous and that the house was located in a spot often passed by raiding Iroquois Indians. As a matter of fact, Indians passed by so frequently that the house in question, the Vercheres's home, was dubbed "Castle Dangerous."

Madeleine Vercheres lived in Quebec during the seventeenth century. Her home was on the St. Lawrence River, and it breathed with an uneasy breath. On the day that Madeleine was left in charge, she was expecting a girlfriend to come to visit her. Her two brothers were playing at the riverside, and a servant was with her. As she watched the river, waiting for her friend's arrival in a boat, two gunshots were heard, and a moment later Madeleine saw about fifty Iroquois marching toward her home.

Quickly gathering her brothers and the servant, Madeleine ran with them towards the nearby fort. Closing the gates on the pursuing Indians, she found to her consternation that there were only two soldiers guarding the fort. Not only that, the two soldiers were very much afraid. Because of Madeleine's insistence, however, they fired a cannon, leading the Indians to believe that there were more people inside the enclosure than just six.

Presently a canoe was sighted on the St. Lawrence. It was Madeleine's friend who had come to visit her. The soldiers refused to leave the relative safety of the fort, so Madeleine opened the door and walked to the dock with a pounding heart. She smiled at her friend, took her arm, and brought her into the fort. She hoped the Indians would think she was a decoy, only tempting them to come closer so that the "army" inside the fort would get a better shot at them. Madeleine's ruse worked, and she and her friend were unharmed.

Under Madeleine's direction, all through that night and the six following days, she, her brothers, her friend, the servant, and the soldiers, cried "All's well" at different times from different locations in the fort. The Indians were convinced there were many people inside and were afraid to come too near.

The seventh day saw help arriving. Madeleine and those with her were rescued. Today, at Vercheres, a village in Quebec which overlooks the St. Lawrence, a bronze statue of Madeleine stands. It is a beautiful statue and seems to inspire people to bravery. But it is not the most beautiful work that was ever created.

* * * * * * *

People have always created statues and painted pictures and carved works of art. In Exodus 35 we read that God filled a man called Bezalel with His Spirit. This was done so that Bezalel might be able to create beautiful, artistic things. Bezalel was filled with the Holy Spirit to create beauty. For, indeed, God loves beautiful things. But that which Bezalel made was not the most beautiful ever created.

O LORD, our Lord,
How excellent is Your name in all the earth,
Who have set Your glory above the heavens!

Out of the mouth of babes and nursing infants
You have ordained strength,
Because of Your enemies,
That You may silence the enemy and the avenger.

When I consider Your heavens, the work of Your fingers,
The moon and the stars, which You have ordained,
What is man that You are mindful of him,
And the son of man that You visit him?

* * * * * * *

There was once a huge block of marble in the city of Florence, Italy. Many sculptors desired to fashion something out of this block of marble. It was eighteen feet high. Within it lay a figure, but who, it was asked, would be able to bring this figure to life? Who would be able to sculpt beauty out of it? A local artist received permission to carve into it, but unfortunately, he was not gifted enough to do a good job. Hacking a great hole into it, he left the block in such a terrible state that it made people weep. It was thought the marble was spoiled and that no one would be able to create anything else out of it.

The block lay sad and useless for many years until, one day, another artist came along. He studied the distorted marble for a long time. He measured and calculated and calculated and measured, and a yearning was born in him to take this block of marble and finish it, to finish it

For You have made him a little lower than the angels,
And You have crowned him with glory and honor.

You have made him to have dominion over the works of
            Your hands;
You have put all things under his feet,
All sheep and oxen—
Even the beasts of the field,
The birds of the air,
And the fish of the sea
That pass through the paths of the seas.

O LORD, our Lord,
How excellent is Your name in all the earth! Psalm 8

even though the gaping hole made it seem as if nothing beautiful was held within it. The young man was given permission by the city to try his hand at working the marble. After all, the city did not have much use for this large chunk of nothing. It was merely taking up room.

The young artist was delighted with the opportunity to sculpt to his heart's content. He sat down and drew on paper the figure he saw hidden in the marble. It was the figure of a young man with a sling in his hand. After he had finished the drawing the young artist set to work. And one of the most beautiful statues of all time was born— the statue of David with a sling in his hand. The sling, the artist said, was a symbol of liberty for the city. It meant that, as David had protected his people and had governed them justly, so whoever ruled Florence should defend and govern that city with justice.

The young artist's name was Michelangelo and the year the statue was finished was 1504. That was a long time ago. Perhaps if every city today would take a statue of David as its symbol, there would be more justice. Or, more to the point, if every city would return to the laws God set forth in the Bible, surely there would be much happiness and rejoicing. Yet, even though this statue of David had a fine reason for being and was truly magnificent to look at, it was not the most beautiful work that was ever created.

* * * * * * *

God is the source of all beauty. Whenever you can praise God for the beauty of a thing, you can be sure that the Spirit of God is present within you. However it does not follow that every artist is automatically a Christian. But because all men were created in the image of God, all men have the ability to express or create beauty.

Then God said, "Let Us make man in Our image, according to Our likeness; let them have dominion over the fish of the sea, over the birds of the air, and over the cattle, over all the earth and over every creeping thing that creeps on the earth. So God created man in His own image; in the image of God He created him; male and female He created them" (Gen. 1:26–27).

And, yes, man was the most beautiful work ever created by an Artist—the Master Artist—because man was created in His own image. It is something we should never forget in an age where abortion and euthanasia are becoming a way of life.

Food For Thought

1. Ephesians 2:10 says, "We are God's workmanship, created in Christ Jesus to do good works, which God prepared in advance

for us to do" (NIV). If God prepared the good works that we are able to do, what should our feelings be when we create something?

2. Why does it comfort you that God, who made the stars in the sky, also takes care of you?

7

Glabori in the Lion's Den

A little less than two thousand years ago, during the years of A.D. 81–98 to be exact, a man named Domitian reigned as Emperor of Rome. When Domitian was a young man, he seems to have been an able ruler. After a series of lost campaigns, however, his outlook changed. Whatever the cause, Domitian became a bitter and cruel emperor. Especially hostile to the Christians in his empire, he persecuted them vigorously. It may have been during this time that the Apostle John was exiled to the island of Patmos, and Timothy, whom we read about in the Bible as well, also suffered during Domitian's reign. Historians say that when Timothy rebuked a pagan procession because they were carrying idols, he was attacked by them with clubs and beaten to death.

Domitian was the first Roman emperor to deify himself by proclaiming to be Lord and God. He hated the Christians because they would not worship him and issued a decree that "no Christian, brought before the emperor's tribunal, should be exempted from punishment without renouncing his religion." In other words, if arrested Christians would bow down to the emperor and acknowledge

So they answered and said before the king, "That Daniel, who is one of the captives from Judah, does not show due regard for you, O king, or for the decree that you have signed, but makes his petition three times a day."

And the king, when he heard these words, was greatly displeased with himself, and set his heart on Daniel to deliver him; and he labored till the going down of the sun to deliver him. Then these men approached the king, and said to the king, "Know, O king, that it is the law of the Medes and Persians that no decree or statute which the king establishes may be changed."

So the king gave the command, and they brought Daniel and cast him into the den of lions. But the king spoke, saying to Daniel, "Your God, whom you serve continually, He will deliver you." Daniel 6:13–16

him as God and swear allegiance to him, they would be set free. But if they did not, they would be killed.

One particular day during the course of Domitian's reign, the amphitheater in Rome, a very large arena, was filled to capacity. Thousands of people—men, women, and children—were crowded into the seats. All were waiting for a prisoner to be led into the arena to be eaten by a ferocious lion. Cages had been built into the side of the amphitheater. These cages were separated from the main arena by huge, sliding, iron doors, and they held starving, wild animals.

Domitian was also at the arena on this particular day. He had the best seat and his view of the arena was better than that of anyone else present. Upon a signal from him, soldiers brought in a young man. A hush fell upon the audience. They had been whispering, fidgeting with the waiting, but the sight of the man quieted and puzzled them to a certain degree. They all knew him. His name was Glabori and, until a short while ago, they had all been in awe of his status. They had all been subject to him because he had been the governor of Rome.

Glabori stood without moving. He silently surveyed the thousands of people surrounding him on all sides. There is no knowing what he actually thought. Only God knows the thoughts of a man's heart. But because he was a recent convert to Christianity, it is almost certain that all his thoughts were fixed upon the Lord, his God. There is almost no doubt that Glabori was praying for strength to be able to endure to the end.

God is a mighty God who hears the prayer of the righteous; God is compassionate toward those who fear Him. God looked upon Glabori with love and helped him. When Domitian gave the signal for the keepers to release a ravenous lion into the arena, Glabori was filled with courage. Not moving at all, he awaited the lion who, only blinking into the harsh sunlight for a few seconds, instantly made for the tall, still figure in the center of the arena. Like a cat about to jump on a mouse, he crouched, quivered, and leaped. And he missed.

Glabori didn't wait for the lion to get ready for a second attack. He threw himself on the beast's back and hung on to the unkempt, yellow mane. The watching crowd was amazed. Half of them rose to their feet. For the space of some thirty seconds Glabori hung on. He pummeled the beast on its sides when he was able, and never fell to the ground. At the end of this time, whether from exhaustion or from divine wounds inflicted by angels, the lion suddenly dropped down. He was dead.

The crowd went wild. They cheered and clapped. Glabori, who stood by the huge, yellow body of the beast that had but moments ago almost killed him, rejoiced. The God in whom he had put his trust had saved him from the mouth of the lion, even as He had saved Daniel before him. According to Roman law, Glabori was now free to go home.

Glabori did go home, but it was only for a few, short days. Domitian, threatened by God's amazing display of power, had him rearrested and beheaded.

Consider, however, just for a moment, the outcome of both men's lives. Domitian was brutally assassinated by conspirators shortly after this. He was only forty-five years old. He had reigned for a small period of fifteen years and would suffer the consequences of his cruel sins for eternity. But Glabori, after a brief earthly struggle, was received by Jesus, his Savior, into glory that was everlasting.

Food For Thought

1. Why is praying before a meal in a restaurant, when you are with other kids who do not believe, the same issue that Daniel faced?

2. Why is turning off a movie, which uses God's name inappropriately, the same issue which Glabori faced?

8

In Danger of Fire

Everyone knows people who have one or two habits that are eccentric, habits that are strange. There are, for example, people who smoke lettuce; Prince Charles of England apparently collects toilets; and I know many people who constantly talk to animals.

Some practices, however, are not only extremely strange but also unexplainable. One of these is the practice of fire walking. Fire walking is done in many different parts of the world, including Japan, North Africa, and some islands in the South Pacific. It is done in one of two ways: either fire walkers stride swiftly over a layer of hot coals spread about in a small ditch; or they walk over stones which have been heated by fire for a number of days. In either case, their pathway is so hot that it can easily burn right through the sole of a thick shoe.

In 1959, an Australian reporter described a fire-walking stunt on Bora Bora, an island in the South Pacific. The people here regarded the practice of fire walking as entertainment. When fire walkers came to a village, everyone gathered around to watch. A fire pit some forty feet long and twenty feet wide was covered with

The coming of the lawless one is according to the work-ing of Satan, with all power, signs, and lying wonders, and with all unrighteous deception among those who perish, be-cause they did not receive the love of the truth, that they might be saved. 2 Thessalonians 2:9–10

rocks lying on a bed of burning wood. This bed was extremely hot because the wood had been kept burning for at least two days prior to the fire walkers' performance. People gave the bed wide berth as the heat that emanated from the rocks was so great that it was impossible to stand close by. The fire walkers let the people in the crowd examine their feet to make sure that they wouldn't be accused of cheating later on by wearing something that protected the soles of their feet. After the foot inspection (and there was no laughter here), the eight fire walkers lined up and picked up palm branches. Singing they began to march, single file, over the pit. Walking briskly and waving their palm branches, they made it to the far end of the pit only to turn around and come back the same way over the same red-hot rocks. When they were done, onlookers were once again permitted to examine their feet. Inspection showed that, although the soles of the feet were black, they had not been burned.

Some small villages in India practice fire walking as a religious ceremony. People do not watch performers but choose to walk through the fire themselves. They think that this practice will prove their faithfulness to the heathen goddess Kali. They hope that by walking through fire, the goddess Kali will perhaps cure them or a friend of a sickness. If parents have a child who is very ill, they will carry that child in their arms through the flames. The people who attempt the fire walking prepare themselves by living in seclusion for a few days before the ceremony. They do not speak to anyone at that time except to those who have already walked through the fire. Although there are people who manage to make the hot walk seven times (the required number for healing and protection), there are many others who are seriously burned. Those who are burned are judged not to have had enough faith.

In the early 1980s, a man by the name of Tolly Burkan claimed that he could teach fire walking in workshops he conducted in the United States. Several thousand people came and went to his classes and are said to have walked on hot coals.

Even though there are people who are injured in this very strange practice, there are also many people who have come through without injury. Scientists are not too clear on how this is possible. Some have suggested that fire walkers have very thick skin. Others say that rapid movement is essential. Still others say that self-hypnosis, applying chemicals to the skin, taking drugs for pain, as well as mystical causes are an aid to fire walkers.

And what are Christians to think of this strange habit or practice? Or rather, does the Bible have any comments to offer? The Bible does tell us that evil is at work in the world and that the work of Satan will be displayed in all kinds of counterfeit miracles, signs, and wonders. It also says that every sort of evil will deceive those who do not believe in God.

It is good to be aware that there is an evil power at work—a power which always tries to undermine the power of God, shamefully copying His power in a distorted manner. This power always tries to rebel against God, and this power fiercely opposes Christ and faith in Him. When we encounter a strange practice, such as fire walking, even if such a practice is far removed from us, it brings us back to basic truths. These truths are threefold. First, that the devil is hard at work in the world; second, that in spite of the devil's hard work, God is in control of the world; and third, that God's ultimate triumph is sure. May His name be praised!

Food For Thought

1. Why do you suppose that people get so excited about strange practices or habits, whereas it seems that the daily wonders of God's providential care seem to pass them by?
2. A miracle can be said to be a "wonder" or a "marvel." What are some of the miracles that you encounter every day?

9

Kate Barlass

She was baptized Catharine Douglas and lived in Scotland about 500 years ago. It was an age of castles and barons, a country of heather and moors, and a time of unrest and war. And during this age of upheaval, when she was still quite young, Catharine became lady-in-waiting to Queen Jane of Scotland, the wife of James I of that country.

Scotland was rife with nobles, many of whom did as they pleased, vying with the king for power. Law and order were not exactly on the daily menu, and the poor were oppressed by baron overlords who taxed, robbed, and terrified them. King James I, pursuing a course of law and order, was not popular with these rough nobles. One of the most powerful families in Scotland at this time was the Douglas family. This family supported James I. Catharine, as a member of this family, was the king's loyal subject and the queen's devoted lady-in-waiting.

One evening in the middle of the winter, as the king and queen, together with some of the queen's maids, were relaxing in front of a fire in a secluded castle chamber, they heard a commotion down the hall. There were angry shouts and noises of fighting. Sending someone out of the room to check, they soon realized that the king's life was being threatened and that one of the power-hungry nobles had broken into the castle with the intent of murdering his sovereign. The guards keeping watch seemed to have been bribed, drugged, or slain.

The small party in the chamber looked at one another in consternation. Their room was deep within the confines of the castle, and the only doorway out was the one through which the assassins would soon inevitably enter. The window in the chamber was heavily barred. The king had no weapons with him, nor did any of the ladies. The outcome seemed certain death.

Suddenly someone remembered that there was a space beneath the wooden floorboards of the room. The noises down the hall steadily grew louder. Clearly there was still some defense, but in a matter of minutes the door would open, the door which all now saw had had its lock broken and its bolt removed. Obviously this treacherous murder had been planned in advance. The king set about tearing the floorboards with the tongs from the fireplace. He worked frantically, while the hearts of all present pounded in their throats.

Catharine noticed at this point in time that the iron rings, which had held the bolt of the door, were just of a size to have a woman put her arm through. She shuddered inwardly and then looked at the faces of the king and queen whom she loved. The queen was panic-stricken, and the king lay on his knees tugging at the floorboards. Catharine's hesitation was only brief. She strode over to the door, holding up her long skirt with one hand. She slipped her right arm through the iron rings. Surely her arm was much weaker than the iron bolt which had lodged there previously, but oh, her arm held more love and compassion than any deadweight thing.

And moreover, because the Preacher was wise, he still taught the people knowledge; yes, he pondered and sought out and set in order many proverbs. The Preacher sought to find acceptable words; and what was written was upright—words of truth. The words of the wise are like goads, and the words of scholars are like well-driven nails, given by one Shepherd. And further, my son, be admonished by these. Of making many books there is no end, and much study is wearisome to the flesh.

Soon the assassins pushed and strained against the door. It vibrated her entire being. The king had loosened the floorboards by now and was lowering himself into the small hold underneath. The weight of what seemed like a thousand men rammed into Catharine's side, but her arm held firm. It gave the queen and the other ladies time to stamp down on the floorboards, pulling rushes over the telltale marks where the king had been working.

Another battering broke Catharine's arm, and she half-fainted as the door was flung open. The room was searched, but there was not much to see. The queen and ladies cowered. No escape was possible from the barred window, and the assassins were baffled. Thinking the king must be in another room, they left to search elsewhere.

Catharine had sunk to the floor. Relieved and in pain, but still fearful, she saw the floorboards lift a minute later as the king's face appeared. The hiding place was extremely cramped, and the oxygen supply was almost nil. Unfortunately, one of the assassins chose that moment to return for a second look. He called out to the others, and James I was brutally stabbed to death.

Scotland was so shocked by this foul murder that it refused to accept Sir Robert Graham, the assassin, as the next king. James's child, a son, succeeded his father.

Let us hear the conclusion of the whole matter:
Fear God and keep His commandments,
For this is man's all.
For God will bring every work into judgment,
Including every secret thing,
Whether good or evil.
Ecclesiastes 12:9–14

* * * * * * *

Catharine's arm had been broken for nothing. Or had it? It must have been very distressing for Catharine to know that, despite her sacrifice, the king was killed. If she was a Christian girl, and we are not told whether she was, she must have been perplexed because what she was doing was so obviously right—she was protecting her monarch. She must have asked God why He had let this happen.

The teacher, or writer of Ecclesiastes, talks about problems such as the one Catharine faced. He saw the enigmas of the world, and he contemplated the meaningless of a lot of actions. Ecclesiastes is not a very long Bible book. It's a good book to read in one sitting. Perhaps Catharine did. And, if she did, she would have found the answer. God has ordered all things (including the opening and barring of doors and the life and death of kings), to happen according to His purpose for reasons we do not always understand. It is our role to accept this and when all is said and done, simply to fear God and to keep His commandments.

History tells us nothing else about Catharine Douglas except for the fact that she was nicknamed Kate Barlass—the lass who barred the door. We can add to that. Even though we don't understand it, we can say she was the lass "used by God" to bar the door. We can

Soon the assassins pushed and strained against the door. The weight of what seemed like a thousand men rammed into Catharine's side, but her arm held firm.

praise His name for seeing that Kate kept one of God's commandments, either knowingly or unknowingly, by being a compassionate servant, ready to do good.

Food For Thought

1. It is not always easy to stand up for someone when they are being bullied by someone else. Do you think that God requires it of us? Why/not?

2. Have you ever seen God's name, or His commandments, under attack? If you did see it, how were you able to "bar the door" for Him in some way?

10

The Girl Who Found Her Life

Perhaps we sometimes take our freedom of worship for granted. We look at the alarm clock on Sunday morning, yawn, turn over in bed and try to stretch the minutes we still have before we rush off to our church service. It has been proven again and again that when things become difficult for Christians, that is to say, when worship services are forbidden, then these worship services become more precious to the believer.

Perpetua, a young woman who lived about 1,800 years ago, greatly joyed in her worship of God with fellow Christians. She thought the fellowship time so valuable that she was willing to be arrested for it.

It was about the year A.D. 200 in the city of Carthage, Africa. The Roman Emperor, Septimus Severus, whose rule extended to Africa, did not particularly care for Christians. It stung his pride that they would not acknowledge him as God. Consequently, he issued warrants of arrest for all those who attended Christian worship services and would not acknowledge him as deity.

Perpetua, who was of noble birth and a new convert to the Christian faith, came from a wealthy, close-knit family. Her parents loved

But Jesus answered them, saying, "The hour has come that the Son of Man should be glorified. Most assuredly, I say to you, unless a grain of wheat falls into the ground and dies, it remains alone; but if it dies, it produces much grain. He who loves his life will lose it, and he who hates his life in this world will keep it for eternal life. If anyone serves Me, let him follow Me; and where I am, there My servant will be also. If anyone serves Me, him My Father will honor. John 12:23–26

her dearly, her husband was devoted to her, and her baby son was sweetness personified. But it grieved Perpetua deeply within her heart that she was the only one in her family who had been found by the Lord. It saddened her tremendously that no one else in her family would have anything to do with the pearl beyond all price.

It was only a matter of time before Perpetua was arrested. Her father, torn between his dislike of Christianity and his love for Perpetua, pleaded with her to deny her faith. "Father," Perpetua told him, "do you see this vase here?" "Yes, I do," he replied. "Could it be called by any other name than what it is?" He answered, "No." "Well, so I too cannot be called by any other name than what I am— a Christian." Although Perpetua spoke these words quietly, they angered her father tremendously. He moved toward her as if to strike her, but thinking better of it, he turned and left her prison cell, disappointment echoing in every step he took.

Perpetua's mother and brother also visited her in prison. She could see sadness in their eyes because they could not comprehend her devotion to something that made her suffer. But somehow the prison she was incarcerated in seemed a palace to her. It was a place where she was able to worship to her heart's delight with fellow believers.

Perpetua's father came to plead with her again. He kissed her hands and threw himself down at her feet. "Have pity on my grey head," he cried. "Do not abandon me to be the reproach of men. Think of your brothers; think of your mother and your aunt; think of your child who will not be able to live once you are gone. Give up your pride! You will destroy all of us! None of us will ever be able to speak freely again if anything happens to you!" Perpetua tried to comfort him. "All things will happen as God wills. You may be sure, father, that no one is left to himself but all people are in His power." But her father would not be comforted with these words and left in great sorrow.

The court hearing took place some days later with the governor of Carthage presiding as judge. When it was Perpetua's turn to stand before him, her father suddenly appeared out of the watching crowd carrying her baby. "Have pity on your father's grey head!" he cried out once more. "Have pity on your infant son. Offer sacrifices for the welfare of the Emperor." Sadly Perpetua replied, "I cannot." The governor then asked her if she was a Christian and she responded, "I am." Because her father continued to try to dissuade her from this, interfering with court procedure, he was ordered beaten. Perpetua herself, together with other Christians, was condemned to death by wild beasts.

On the day they were to die Perpetua and her fellow Christians walked calmly to the arena. Perpetua sang a psalm as she walked, and it is said that everyone who looked at her was shamed into turning their gazes away. Others in her group warned the onlookers: "You have condemned us. Take care that God will not condemn you." At this the crowd became enraged and demanded that the Christians be scourged before they died. And this was done.

Perpetua and a young slave girl named Felicitas were the only two women in the group. Shamefully stripped naked, they were the first two taken into the arena to be killed. Placed in a net, they were thus carried to their place of execution. The crowd was temporarily moved when they saw that Felicitas was only a young girl and that

Perpetua was not much older. Because of the crowd's compassion the two girls were taken back and dressed in unbelted tunics. At their second entrance into the arena, a mad heifer charged at them, wounding both girls. Bleeding, Perpetua was thrown to the ground, but she was able to rise and walk toward Felicitas. Carefully she put her arm around the younger girl and helped her stand. When the people saw them standing together, arms around one another, they again had a brief moment of compassion and shouted that these girls should be killed in a kinder fashion—by sword rather than by wild beasts.

Thus it happened that the Christian men were killed first. Then Perpetua and Felicitas were led back into the arena for a third time. Both finally obtained the martyr's crown by the sword of a gladiator.

And Jesus said, "He who loves father or mother more than Me is not worthy of Me. And he who loves son or daughter more than Me is not worthy of Me. And he who does not take his cross and follow after Me is not worthy of Me. He who finds his life will lose it, and he who loses his life for My sake will find it" (Matthew 10:37–39).

Food For Thought

1. Have you ever not wanted to go to church? Or, have you ever tried to get out of going to church? If a law was passed that said that going to church was punishable by imprisonment, would you end up in prison? Why/not?
2. The Bible tells us that children are to obey their parents. Perpetua disobeyed hers. Was this correct? Why/not?

11

Maewyn's Vision

Maewyn Sucat was born in Wales around the year 389. The Romans ruled Great Britain at this time, and Maewyn was proud of his nationality. His people built fine churches and sturdy houses. Calpurnius Sucat, Maewyn's father, was a magistrate, a Roman official. He was also a deacon in the Christian church. Calpurnius and his wife taught Maewyn about God. But although Maewyn listened with his ears, his heart was stopped up. He had no need of the Gospel. He led a sheltered existence. There were servants to obey him, plenty of food, a strong roof over his head, and fine clothes to wear.

Across the sea from England lay the country of Ireland. Ireland was ruled by a number of powerful men. Each man called himself a king and the most powerful of them all was King Niall. But even more powerful than the kings were the Druid priests. With power to declare war and make peace, practicing divination and sorcery, these Druid priests often resorted to human sacrifice. When Maewyn was sixteen years old, King Niall, with the Druids' encouragement, attacked England and took thousands of prisoners. Maewyn was one of these prisoners. Taken away from friends and family, he was sold into slavery to one of the rulers of Ireland. Suddenly there were no more servants to bring him his dinner; no fresh clothes were laid out for him in the morning; and the roof over his head was exchanged for the great outdoors. From heir to a rich house, Maewyn was demoted to the position of swineherd.

Sometimes when our luxuries are taken away from us, we begin to appreciate things more and more. So it was with Maewyn. Alone in a strange country, with plenty of time on his hands to think about why he had been pirated away from his home and friends, he found that the only comfort he had was in prayer. In his loneliness, Maewyn was thrown into the arms of God. He prayed much and such is the power of prayer that it made a child a man and the man a child of God.

After he had lived in Ireland for six years, Maewyn had a vision in which he heard a voice saying to him, "Behold, a ship is ready for thee." He got up, left the swine, and walked many miles to the sea. No one stopped him. Finding a ship, he secured a passage and was taken to an island off the southern coast of France. Here he entered a monastery and seriously began to study the Bible.

When Maewyn, after an absence of nearly ten years, returned to the village where he had been born, his family was overjoyed to see him. For a while he was happy to be back, but one night he was given another dream. In it a man spoke to him and said, "Why dost thou loiter here in peace and happiness when there are men waiting in darkness for a message from God that thou shouldst carry to them? Arise and return to the land of thy captivity, for the people there need thee."

Maewyn was certain God was calling him to go back to Ireland. In the year 432 he was ordained as missionary and renamed Patricius. Joyfully, Patricius, or Patrick, sailed back to Ireland. He had eight fellow workers with him to face the enmity of the Druid priests and to help him preach. He prayed much and earnestly.

Patrick thought that if the kings of Ireland would be converted to Christ, surely the tribe members would follow. At this time the high

> *Then He said: "A certain man had two sons. And the younger of them said to his father, 'Father, give me the portion of good that falls to me.' So he divided to them his livelihood. And not many days after, the younger son gathered all together, journeyed to a far country, and there wasted his possessions with prodigal living. But when he had spent all, there arose a severe famine in that land, and he began to be in want. Then he went and joined himself to a citizen of that country, and he sent him into his fields to feed swine. And he would gladly have filled his stomach with the pods that the swine ate, and no one gave him anything.*

king of Ireland was a man named Laager. Legend has it that as Patrick spoke to Laager in the name of the Lord, the chief Druid continually mocked Patrick and his God. But as he mocked, a lightning bolt struck him down and stunned him while an earthquake rocked the countryside. Believing in Patrick's God, many were converted, and Laager is reported to have said, "Thy God is great and wonderful. He has worked miracles for thee. Thou mayest indeed carry thy message to the people of my kingdom, and I will help thee as I may."

Although there were people who hated Patrick and tried to kill him, God protected him. His success was amazing. He traveled, preached, converted, and baptized. The King of Leinster, the King of Munster, and many others came to Christ until it was said that Ireland had more Christians per square mile than any other country. With God's help, Patrick established monasteries and schools. The Irish tribes did not yet have a written language, but the gift of the Christian religion gave them the Latin alphabet. Gospel books Patrick carried with him became Irish treasures. Students spent their lives copying them, and Irish monasteries became the cradles of many who would later spread the Gospel throughout Europe.

> *"But when he came to himself, he said, 'How many of my father's hired servants have bread enough and to spare, and I perish with hunger! I will arise and go to my father, and will say to him, "Father, I have sinned against heaven and before you, and I am no longer worthy to be called your son. Make me like one of your hired servants."'*
>
> *"And he arose and came to his father. But when he was still a great way off, his father saw him and had compassion, and ran and fell on his neck and kissed him."*
> *(Luke 15:11–20)*

When Patrick died on March 17 (the year is thought to be 461), he was buried at Downpatrick in Ireland. After his death, the Roman Catholic Church attributed many miracles to him and permitted people to pray to him. They maintain that he got rid of all the poisonous snakes in Ireland by beating a drum. They say he made snow burn and that he raised his father from the dead. We know, however, that Patrick was only a man, and that, like all men, he was here to praise God. We should, therefore, never sing praises to Patrick or pray to Patrick, but we should pray to Patrick's God, who permitted Patrick (and us) to preach His salvation.

Food For Thought

1. If you were taken away from your home, friends, and all the security you have known, do you think that your faith would grow stronger? Why/not?

2. Does it require as much courage to cross the seas to preach the Gospel to strangers, as it does to go across the street to preach to neighbors? How so?

12

Coelacanth

In the month of December in the year 1938, a trawler was fishing off the coast of Madagascar. When the owner of the boat pulled in the net, a strange-looking fish was seen among all the other fish. It was a fisherman's dream, a creature all of six feet long with a very oily skin. Along with the other fish in the catch, the whopping wriggler was taken to market. Perhaps, the fisherman reasoned, someone would pay good money for such a large fish.

A naturalist happened to be out shopping for a fish supper that day. She stopped, examined the fish, and bought it without haggling about the price. This was because she realized during her examination that the man-sized creature in the fishmonger's stall was special. Time proved her to be correct. The giant fish was identified as a coelacanth (pronounced see-la-kanth).

A coelacanth? Now hold on a moment. The coelacanth was supposed to be extinct. Its petrified skeleton had previously been found in rock which had been dated by scientists to be at least seventy million years old. Coelacanth fossils had been found for years and years, and everyone was completely convinced that it was a fish that

> *Then God said, "Let the waters abound with an abun-dance of living creatures, and let birds fly above the earth across the face of the firmament of the heavens." So God cre-ated great sea creatures and every living thing that moves, with which the waters abounded, according to their kind, and every winged bird according to its kind. And God saw that it was good. And God blessed them, saying, "Be fruitful and multiply, and fill the waters in the seas, and let birds multiply on the earth." So the evening and the morning were the fifth day. Genesis 1:20–23*

used to be—a fish that was extinct. It could not just be lying there, six feet long, among other fish in a twentieth-century fish market.

Most public schools teach children about an evolutionary tree of life. It shows them a diagram depicting how different forms of life started and how these forms of life changed, becoming better and better. The tree ends with a monkey evolving into man. The coela-canth is also a part of this tree. It serves as a link between fish and amphibians. It is supposed to be the first fish that, emerging out of the water, began to crawl and then to walk.

There is no doubt that the coelacanth is quite an unusual fish. The special hinge in its head allows it to open its mouth enormously wide to feed. And, unlike most fish, the coelacanth does not lay eggs, but bears live young. It also seems to be able to give off weak electric charges to help it maneuver through dark, rough slopes. The coelacanth is, indeed, a marvelous creation!

Does the coelacanth prove evolution, though? On the contrary! If you compare the fossil of a dead coelacanth (supposedly millions of years old), to a live coelacanth (at least thirty have been caught since 1938), you will find out that they are as alike as the proverbial two peas in a pod.

Obviously the coelacanth is a creature according to its own kind and did not evolve into another crawling or walking type of creature. Genesis 1:21 tells us, "So God created great sea creatures and every living thing that moves, with which the waters abounded, according to their kind . . ."

The coelacanth, much to the disappointment of the evolutionist, is not an evolutionary link at all. If you discover a coelacanth fossil someday with the imprint of its wonderful six-foot body, this will tell you only one thing. It will tell you that "kinds" as God created them, remain basically the same. Take a dog—have you ever heard it cheep? Have you, for that matter, ever heard a cat bark? Or a pig moo?

First Corinthians 15:38–39 tell us that God "to each kind of seed . . . gives its own body. All flesh is not the same: Men have one kind of flesh, animals have another, birds another and fish another." The flesh of the six-foot coelacanth fish had many details and characteristics given to it by God. Distinctive patterns of white spots as camouflage help it blend in with white sponges on the seafloor. And with its spotted body the coelacanth swims strangely—sometimes backwards, sometimes belly-up. But it never crawls or walks. The reason for that is very simple. God did not create the coelacanth as an amphibian—He created the coelacanth as a fish. And He created it on the fifth day, not millions of years ago.

Food For Thought

1. Genesis 1:5 says, "God called the light Day, and the darkness He called Night. So the evening and the morning were the first

day." Verses 8, 13, 19, 23, and 31 all repeat the same refrain, "So the evening and the morning were the second day . . . , the third day . . . , the fourth day . . . , the fifth day . . . , and the sixth day." What would you say if someone told you that God created the world through evolution, and that each of the six days of creation were a few million years?

2. Why do you suppose that people believe in evolution?

13

Even Inventors Die

The baby in the cradle appeared so puny, so like a shrunken, little man, that most of the visitors at Mrs. Edison's bedside felt sorry for her. *Poor dear,* they thought, *baby Thomas doesn't look very strong. It's not likely she'll hold him in her arms very long. It's not likely he will live.*

In spite of these gloomy predictions, however, Thomas did live and he grew. He grew to ask so many questions that his father was sure Thomas's tongue was the shape of a question mark. "Why is the sky blue? Why does grass grow out of the ground? Why is rain wet?"

Milan, Ohio, the place where Thomas grew up, was a busy town. A canal connected it to the Huron River. Many people came by— carpenters, ship owners, and trades people. Young Thomas asked them all questions. He fell into the canal one day and almost drowned. As he was fished out, water running from his hair and eyes, not at all perturbed by the jeopardy he had been in, he asked, "Why is the water that color?"

Thomas Edison was hungry for knowledge. He had a great desire within him to know how things worked. "Why does a goose sit on a nest, mother?" "So her eggs will keep warm, Thomas." "Why?"

> *As you do not know what is the way of the wind,*
> *Or how the bones grow in the womb of her who is with*
> *child,*
> *So you do not know the works of God who makes every-*
> *thing. Ecclesiastes 11:5*

"So they will hatch, Thomas." "What does hatching mean?" "That's when the goslings come out of the shell." "Do they come out because the goose makes it warm?" "Yes, Thomas." Thomas thought a great deal about this conversation. He sat down and watched the goose. He watched for a long time but was disappointed that the goslings did not emerge. Finally he decided that, since he was bigger than the goose, he could speed things up a little. He chased the goose away and sat down on the eggs. As the eggs cracked and his pants became soggy, he realized that, although he had made a goose of himself, he would never be able to hatch eggs.

When Thomas was seven, his family moved to Port Huron, Michigan. Because his report card was below par and did not reflect the abilities she knew he had, Mrs. Edison decided that she would teach her son at home. She and Thomas set up a laboratory in the cellar. They found a chemistry book which described all sorts of experiments and began to study. Thomas tried all the experiments. He learned how acids affect materials. He found out how wheels turn in the pendulum of a clock. He built two machines to generate electricity, and he made paper dolls dance by electric shocks.

When the railroad came to Michigan, Thomas was hired for work on the train between Detroit and Port Huron. He was only twelve years old. The ride to Detroit took three hours, and during that time Thomas sold newspapers and candy to the people on the train. In time, he transferred much of the cellar laboratory to one of

During his lifetime, Thomas Alva Edison invented over 1,000 things.

the train cars. This allowed him to use part of the train ride for conducting experiments. One day, however, the train jumped a piece of track and a phosphorus spill caused a fire. The conductor came running. Fortunately, the fire was doused. But Thomas and all his equipment were thrown off the train at the next stop. It was back to the cellar for young Mr. Edison.

One day as Thomas strolled about the railway yard, he saw the station-master's infant son crawling on the tracks. A train was on the way. Thomas ran onto the tracks, grabbed the boy, and saved him in the nick of time. The father was so grateful, he taught Thomas telegraphy (sending messages through a telegraph). It gave Thomas a trade, and as a young lad he worked in many cities as a telegrapher.

In 1869, Edison traveled to New York. He was penniless. A friend gave him permission to sleep in one of the rooms of a gold stock ticker company. (A stock ticker was a machine used to report the price of gold.) The stock ticker broke, and when no one else was able to fix it, Thomas did. He was then offered a job at that particular company at $300 a month. Edison continued to make such marvelous improvements on the stock ticker that eventually the president of the company offered him $40,000 for the patent.

With the $40,000, Edison set up his own laboratory in Menlo Park, New Jersey. Here he was able to invent all day long to his heart's content. He also married but did not see much of his family as he sometimes worked forty to fifty hours straight. He had become deaf as a teenager. An operation could have cured him of this malady, but he did not want to have the surgery. Deafness, he said, made it easier for him to concentrate on his experiments.

During his lifetime, Thomas Alva Edison invented over one thousand things. Our lives are affected by many of them. When we turn on a light (light bulb), or play a record (phonograph), or watch a movie (moving pictures), we are using things Thomas Edison invented.

There is no doubt that Thomas Edison was a great inventor. But there is an inventor even greater than Edison. This inventor created things that Edison could not begin to understand. Job 9:7-10 speaks of this inventor when it says, "He commands the sun, and it does not rise; He seals off the stars; He alone spreads out the heavens, and treads on the waves of the sea; He made the Bear, Orion, and the Pleiades, and the chambers of the south; He does great things past finding out, yes, wonders without number" (NIV).

Edison was not known to be a religious man. He believed in something which he referred to as the Supreme Intelligence. He also was very well aware that, although he could invent many, many things, there was one thing he could not invent—and that was life. Thomas was fascinated by life after death. Reverting back to his childhood, he again asked a question—probably the most important one of his life: "Is death the end?" During his lifetime he never discovered the answer to that question, although when he grew older he tried very hard to invent something that would possibly pick up evidence of life after death. Because he did not use the Textbook of Textbooks as a starting point, he did not, of course, succeed.

Thomas died in 1931. He lies buried in a coffin, in a cemetery, and his body has deteriorated to dust. And the Textbook which Thomas did not study, the Bible, tells us that his soul will have been judged by the greatest inventor of all, God Almighty, the Creator of the universe in which Edison lived for such a short space of time.

Food For Thought

1. If Thomas had studied the Bible as faithfully as he studied chemistry books, perhaps he would have been able to answer

the question he had about death. Can you answer it? Check John 11:25.

2. Why do you think that inventing things, creating new things, might make people think too highly of themselves? What can you do to prevent pride?

14

Weeping May Tarry the Night, But Joy Comes in the Morning

Very often it is in times of greatest sorrow, in moments of deepest woe, that beautiful things are written and that true values are realized.

During the mid-1600s, the little village of Eilenburg in Saxony[*] suffered through some very difficult times. It had been caught up in the Thirty Years' War[†] and in a short period of just eighteen years was overrun by the Swedes twice and the Austrians once. Because of these three devastating invasions, out of the thousand homes standing in the small village, almost eight hundred had been destroyed. Crops had been ruined by passing troops, and famine was sadly evident in the round, hunger bellies of the village children. Mothers had little to cook, and fathers found it hardly worthwhile to work fields that would very likely only be ravaged by hungry soldiers again come harvest time.

[*] Division of North Germany with varying boundaries ruled by an Elector (a German prince).

[†] A series of wars (1618–1648) in central Europe involving a number of countries.

I will extol you, O Lord, for You have lifted me up,
And have not let my foes rejoice over me.
O Lord my God, I cried out to You,
And You healed me.
O Lord, You brought my soul up from the grave;
You have kept me alive, that I should not go down to the pit.

As if that wasn't enough trouble, homeless refugees from nearby areas carried the plague to Eilenburg. Four times that scourge swept through the village. If a family had not lost someone through a bayonet wound, then very likely that family would have lost someone in the plague. It was a hard and difficult time—a time of death and tears.

There was only one minister left in the area. The rest had all died or fled. The minister's name was Martin Rinkhart. There were days when Pastor Martin Rinkhart was called on to bury as many as fifty people! Many parents lost all their children in the space of a few, small hours, and many children became orphans. The smell of illness and death lurked in every corner of Eilenburg. Pastor Rinkhart had to do much comforting, and sometimes his own tears would not stop flowing. As a matter of fact, he could only keep up his hectic pace of pastoral care by studying the Word of God diligently in the free moments he had. Passages like 2 Corinthians 1:3–4 encouraged him: "Praise be to the God and Father of our Lord Jesus Christ, the Father of compassion and the God of all comfort, Who comforts us in all our troubles, so that we can comfort those in any trouble with the comfort we ourselves have received from God" (NIV).

In 1648 the Peace of Westphalia* was signed. The war was finally over. People were ecstatic and danced and hugged each other

---

* Treaty ending the Thirty Years' War.

Sing praise to the LORD, you saints of His,
And give thanks at the remembrance of His holy name.
For His anger is but for a moment,
His favor is for life;
Weeping may endure for a night,
But joy comes in the morning. Psalm 30:1–5

in what was left of the streets of Eilenburg. They could visualize grain in their barren fields; they could see their fallen houses rebuilt; and they hoped against hope that their skeleton children would once more become rosy-cheeked and sturdy. The Elector of Saxony ordered Thanksgiving services in every church of the province including the church of Eilenburg. He also requested that every pastor preach from a text that he would provide.

When Martin Rinkhart received the words provided by the Elector, he carefully read them. "Now bless ye the God of all, who everywhere doeth great things, who exalteth our days from the womb and dealeth with us according to His mercy. May he grant us joyful hearts, and may peace be in our days forever."[*] Leaning back in his study chair, Martin Rinkhart sighed. In his mind's eye he could see yesterday's smoke from burning fields; he could literally hear the wailing at the gravesides; and with the hand that held his quill he could feel the bones of the thin village children.

Recalling himself to the present, he got up and looked out of his window onto the fields; fields that were once more being worked by the local farmers. He heard laughter from the street, and he saw some children playing with a ball almost as round as their bellies had been. He heard a lark sing in the apple trees. And Martin

---

[*] The Elector likely paraphrased some of the words of Psalm 72:18 and Psalm 22:9–10.

Rinkhart lifted up his eyes to the sky and prayed because he was filled with such peace and with such thankfulness that God had given him and the village this hard time. For Martin knew that they could now doubly appreciate all the goodness they had. He understood with his inner being that weeping may tarry the night, but always, always, God gives joy to His people in the morning.

The thankfulness which Martin felt flowed from his pen onto a sheet of paper. He was moved to write a hymn, one which we still sing today, and he let his congregation sing it in the Thanksgiving service the Elector of Saxony had ordained. The words to the hymn read:

> *Now thank we all our God*
> *with hearts and hands and voices,*
> *Who wondrous things has done,*
> *in whom this world rejoices;*
> *Who from our mothers' arms,*
> *hath blessed us on our way*
> *with countless gifts of love,*
> *and still is ours today.*

Food For Thought

1. Do you think people love something more, or count it dearer, if they have almost lost it? Why/not?
2. Do you think that experiencing a difficult time might be good for you or for your church? Why/not?

15

Who Gives Birth to the Frost?

Many years ago, a Jewish mother walked through a forest. She carried a baby girl on her hip, and a black-haired boy held onto her hand. They walked fast—as fast as the small boy's legs could go. German soldiers searched for them not too far behind. It was cold out and rain began to fall. The woman began to walk faster, pulling the child along. Glancing behind her, she saw their tell-tale footprints clearly outlined in the soft ground. Those footprints would surely guide the soldiers straight to them. The boy stumbled, and she picked him up too. Weariness overwhelmed her as she looked ahead at the unending line of black trees. But in the distance she suddenly also discerned the light of a small cottage, almost hidden in the rain. With no idea of who lived there, she plodded toward it. Branches creaked ominously. Every sound brought more anxiety. Reaching the cottage, the woman knocked timidly. The door opened and an old man motioned her in. She and her children were fed and given a place to sleep. And no soldier found the door to that cottage. The rain, you see, changed to snow—heavy, thick snow. The tracks were obliterated. God had hidden both the woman and her children in the cottage.

> *Have you entered the treasury of snow,*
> *Or have you seen the treasury of hail,*
> *Which I have reserved for the time of trouble,*
> *For the day of battle and war?*
> *By what way is light diffused,*
> *Or the east wind scattered over the earth?*
>
> *Who has divided a channel for the overflowing water,*
> *Or a path for the thunderbolt,*
> *To cause it to rain on a land where there is no one,*

Weather is a strange thing. Scientists like to think that sooner or later they will be able to control it completely. As a matter of fact, people have been allowed to discover techniques in which several weather conditions can be controlled. For example, it is possible at times to make a cloud burst to produce rainfall over parched areas. Machines have also been invented which produce artificial snow for winter sports. People like to be in control. They like to be able to say ahead of time, "Tomorrow will be cool," or, "Scattered showers are predicted," because many activities are planned around the weather.

God has given us a wealth of signs about weather in the nature around us. People did not always have the six o'clock news and weather report, or newspapers with an extended forecast. (Mind you, these reports and forecasts are sometimes wrong.) For many years almanacs were (and still are) useful. An almanac is a guide with a weather calendar in it. This calendar is based on moon positions. Different moon positions mean different weather conditions.

The almanac observes how animals behave and how they build their homes. Listen to this 1733 almanac rhyme:

A wilderness in which there is no man;
To satisfy the desolate waste,
And cause to spring forth the growth of tender grass?
Has the rain a father?
Or who has begotten the drops of dew?
From whose womb comes the ice?
And the frost of heaven, who gives it birth?
The waters harden like stone,
And the surface of the deep is frozen.
        Job 38:22–30

Observe which way the hedgehog builds her nest
        To front the north or south or east or west
For if 'tis true what common people say,
        The wind will blow the quite contrary way.

Beekeepers have observed that bees are weather prophets also. When bees stay close to the hive, rain is near. Even cows are signs of weather. Listen to this bit of cute wisdom:

A cow with its tail to the west, makes weather the best;
A cow with its tail to the east, makes weather the least.

Jesus also acknowledged the weather signs His Father had put in nature. He tells us in Luke 12:54–55, "Whenever you see a cloud rising out of the west, immediately you say, 'A shower is coming'; and so it is. And when you see the south wind blow, you say, 'There will be hot weather'; and there is."

The weatherman uses instruments such as a barometer (for measuring air pressure) and a hygrometer (for measuring humidity). But there are many ordinary things around us that we ourselves can also use. These are sounds, sights, feelings, and smells that God has built into our surroundings. Some of them are very interesting and helpful to know. When the air is very moist, the beams in a barn will swell and creak. You can also actually hear bad weather coming. Far away sounds seem to become more clear. Distant bird calls might sound hollow. Elijah, in the Bible, knew that too. Remember the drought in his time? When God's rain finally came, Elijah said in 1 Kings 18:41, "There is the sound of abundance of rain." Some people feel the weather change. Perhaps they have old wounds and scar tissue reacting to pressure in the air. The almanac says:

> *A coming storm your shooting corns presage*
> *And aches will throb, your hollow tooth will rage.*

One natural little instrument which we have, one which the weatherman does not use, is the cricket. Crickets are actually just like little thermometers. They chirp faster when they are warm and slower when they are cold. If you count their chirps for fourteen seconds, then add forty, you will have calculated the approximate temperature of wherever the cricket is.

Weather covers many aspects of our lives. People often joke about the weather.

Knock, knock.
Who's there?
August.
August who?
August of wind.

Or:

What's worse than raining cats and dogs?
Hailing taxi cabs.

Yes, these are groaners. But seriously, it does us good to think of who holds the weather and its signs in His hand. God spoke to Job about His total control over all of nature. Read Job 38:22–30 often to remind yourself of it. It's a beautiful passage. Remember Joshua's battle in which the sun stood still? In that same battle God let large hailstones fall down from the sky, and "there were more who died from the hailstones than the children of Israel killed with the sword." (Josh. 10:11b).

When Jesus calmed the storm on a lake, the disciples correctly were in awe of Him. They said, "Who can this be? For He commands even the winds and water, and they obey Him!" (Luke 8:25b). Our God is the Creator of heaven and earth. He's got the whole world in His hands and that certainly includes the weather. He held it in the beginning. He holds it now, and He will hold it into eternity.

Food For Thought

1. Have you ever watched the thunder and lightning during a really big storm? What were your feelings and thoughts at the time?
2. During Elijah's time God used the weather to punish His people for turning away from Him. Why do you think that He might, or might not, do such a thing today also?

16

Betrayal and Loyalty

There is no feeling so horrendous, so miserable, as having a friend do something that disappoints you. When I was little, I had a girl-friend whom I loved with all the passion a seven year old can muster. The day that she stole one of my toys, and lied about it with a straight face, broke the confidence I had in her. It wasn't that I wanted my toy back. I wanted an unsullied friendship back—I wanted to be able to love her in the same way again. I was disappointed in human nature. It was part of growing up.

Everyone has stories of disappointment, of meeting failures in friends, and of being failures and disappointments themselves.

* * * * * * *

There was a man of God who was born in 1492 in North Nibley, Gloucestershire, England. He was no discoverer of new lands but a translator of old words. His name was William Tyndale. Born into an era when the church of Rome continually disappointed people by betraying their faith, Tyndale became a priest, one who wanted to

> *And while He was still speaking, behold, a multitude;*
> *and he who was called Judas, one of the twelve, went before*
> *them and drew near to Jesus to kiss Him. But Jesus said to*
> *him, "Judas, are you betraying the Son of Man with a kiss?"*
> Luke 22:47–48

stay loyal to the faith portrayed in the Bible. He wanted others to be loyal to that faith also, and this is why he vowed that he would translate the Bible into English proper.

Living at a time when most priests gambled and drank, Tyndale's desire to translate the Bible was seen as a threat. God's Word would expose traitors, because it would show that most priests did not live as they should. When Tyndale was refused the church's permission to translate the Bible in England, he sailed across the sea to Germany. He was poor, but there were merchants who helped him, providing him with a home in which to live and food to eat. Tyndale translated the New Testament and, with the help of the same merchants, shipped thousands of copies back to England. His heart's desire was to give everyone the opportunity to read of God's mercy and love. Even though the risk of owning a Bible was punishable by torture and even death, many people in England came and bought a New Testament.

The church now put a price on Tyndale's head. He did not return to England but stayed in Germany. He reworked the New Testament to make it a better translation and began work on the Old Testament. It is not precisely known in which city he did his work. Years later, in 1534, believing it would finally be safe for him to come out of hiding, Tyndale settled in Antwerp, Belgium. He continued his writing and was also busy with other good works, saying, "My part be not in Christ if mine heart be not to follow and live according as

I teach." Mondays he spent ministering to immigrants who had fled England because of persecution, and Saturdays saw him seeking Antwerp's alleys and doorways for the poor. When a man by the name of Henry Phillips came to Tyndale's room one day asking, "Can I borrow forty shillings, kind sir, for I have lost my purse?" Tyndale lent the money to him cheerfully. Appearing overwhelmed by Tyndale's generosity, Phillips bowed and said, "Mr. Tyndale, I must repay you for this kindness. Please be my guest for dinner." "No, indeed," Tyndale responded, "you shall be my guest." He put on his cloak, and the two went down from Tyndale's room to the street. Conversing in a friendly manner with the man, Tyndale walked through a narrow alley right into a trap. Phillips, who had been hired by the English bishops, had posted soldiers to arrest the translator. Betrayed, Tyndale was taken to a prison in the castle of Vilvorde, some eighteen miles from Antwerp.

Betrayal is an awful thing. No doubt, Tyndale must have felt sick, kicked in the stomach by a man who had been jovial and sincere one minute and hateful and unloving the next. Sitting in the damp and chilly prison cell the next day, he must have wondered why he had not felt distrust, or why he had not sensed the man's dishonesty.

Tyndale did not despair, however. He knew that, although he was in prison, the words he had translated would set many free from the bonds of sin. In his cell he talked unceasingly about his Lord and Savior to anyone who would listen. During the eighteen months he was kept there, his witness was so strong that the prison guard and other members of the castle household were converted.

After eighteen months in prison, Tyndale was condemned as a heretic. His only crime had been loyalty to Jesus' Great Commission: a desire to have fellow countrymen read the Bible. On Friday, October 6, 1536, he was led to a cross. The cross, fashioned by two huge beams, had a chain and a rope hanging from it. Tyndale was chained to the cross and strangled with the rope before his body burned. He was only forty-four years old.

Approximately fifteen centuries before Tyndale's death, someone else died who was also betrayed. And surely this betrayal was the worst betrayal that ever was, making all other betrayals nothing in comparison. Jesus was "oppressed and He was afflicted, yet He opened not His mouth; He was led as a lamb to the slaughter, and as a sheep before its shearers is silent, so He opened not His mouth" (Isaiah 53:7). Jesus was betrayed for us. He suffered the awful pain and death of the cross and remained loyal to His chosen people. His death is an example to us and a great comfort. For when Jesus died "He bore the sin of many, and made intercession for the transgressors" (Isaiah 53:12b).

Food For Thought

1. Is disobedience during the absence of parents or teachers a betrayal of confidence? Have you ever done it?
2. If you were betrayed and arrested for the sake of your faith in Jesus Christ, would there be enough evidence to convict you? What would the evidence be?

17

With All My Love

February 14 is Valentine's Day—a day in which people send each other cards and candy and flowers. Many seem to have a need to express love for each other in some sort of tangible way. Companies, of course, take advantage of this time of the year and put out all sorts of cards and cute gadgets that people can buy to give to their sweethearts. They do a booming business.

Love is a wonderful thing. It's something that makes you happy. It's a feeling that makes you want to sing and shout. One sappy card I ran across read:

This is the day birds choose their mates
And I choose you if I'm not too late.

Perhaps all true love that has been crossed with some sort of difficulty becomes more dear, more precious, as it were. Stories abound of lovers who have encountered hardship, stories that tug at our heartstrings, stories such as Shakespeare's Romeo and Juliet.

It is recorded that in the 1800s, in Bromfield, England, there

> *And as they were eating, Jesus took bread, blessed and broke it, and gave it to the disciples and said, "Take, eat; this is My body."*
>
> *Then He took the cup, and gave thanks, and gave it to them, saying, "Drink from it, all of you. For this is My blood of the new covenant, which is shed for many for the remission of sins. But I say to you, I will not drink of this fruit of the vine from now on until that day when I drink it new with you in My Father's kingdom." Matthew 26:26–29*

lived a young girl who fell in love, head over heels, with a young man in the neighboring village of Downton. He was a stalwart young man who loved the girl in return. After courting her for a number of months, the young man finally worked up enough courage to ask his sweetheart's father for her hand in marriage. The father, however, for whatever reason, did not approve of the match. He refused point-blank to give his consent for the marriage. The girl was heartbroken. She wept and pleaded and pleaded and wept, but her father would not relent. She finally said, "I will do anything you ask, Father—anything—if only you will give your consent." "All right," the father answered, "I will give my consent if you will crawl on your hands and knees on the ground from your home here in Bromfield to your sweetheart's home in Downton. If you do that," and here he laughed, never thinking that his daughter would take him seriously, "you can have this young man for your husband."

The father, however, in saying these words, had unwisely underestimated the power of his daughter's love. The girl crawled for a whole day and half a night; she crawled while pebbles and dirt ate into her kneecaps and shins; and she crawled on as her hands became bruised and bleeding. She stayed on all fours until she reached

The girl crawled for a whole day and half a night; she stayed on all fours until she reached a meadow not far from Downton. The girl was willing to humble herself to a great extent for the man she loved.

a meadow not far from Downton. Exhausted and hungry, she lay in the grass of the meadow and her father, who had been following his daughter's progress in amazement, was overcome with pity at this point and gave his consent for the nuptials. To this day, by the village of Downton, England, there is a meadow called Crawl Meadows, and it testifies to the strong love a person can exhibit for someone else.

The girl in this story was willing to humble herself to a great extent for the man she loved. She was willing to suffer pain for him so that she could marry him. It's a nice story and illustrates well the fact that love is giving. For her, though, it was also going to be receiving. For all the crawling she had done, she was going to receive a reward, and that reward was marriage.

There is also a story of another place that testifies to a greater love than Crawl Meadows. It is a place to which someone walked for the sake of love. Someone who loved but was not loved in return. That place was Golgotha, the place of the Skull. The person was Jesus Christ who stumbled under the heavy load of the cross; Jesus Christ who was killed because he loved His own with such a great love.

Perhaps someone should invent Good Friday cards. Surely they are of much greater significance than Valentine's Day cards!

Food For Thought

1. Do you think your parents experience pain and hardship to feed, clothe, educate, and discipline you? Why/not?
2. Would you be willing to experience pain or hardship so that someone you loved could benefit? What if you were not loved in return? Can we ever love in the same way as Jesus loves His children?

18

Gullible and Foolish

Do you think that you're gullible? I know that I am. Actually, the truth of the matter is that most people can be tricked. Most people have had a joke played on them at some point or other in time.

In the 1930s, a reporter for a paper, perhaps bored by the dismal and despairing news of an ongoing depression, wrote about a fictitious farmer whom he named Lester Green. He made Lester Green out to be as intelligent (or silly) as people would swallow, and they were able to swallow a lot. For example, he had Lester come up with a solution for starting a cold car engine when temperatures were low. Put two setting hens on the car hood, he advised, and you'll have no trouble on a cold morning. Because a hen's temperature is 102, it naturally follows that the temperature of two hens is 204. Buy two chickens and start your car. Would you have believed Lester Green? Read on—many, many people were sitting ducks, and were gullible enough to trust and believe this country adviser.

Farmer Green was next lauded as having isolated a fluid in pigs that made their tails curl. His wife and daughter, he reported, just happened to rub this fluid into their hair and, wonder of wonders, overnight their hair curled. This strange bit of news engendered bags and bags of mail. Please, people wrote, tell us where we can buy this pig fluid.

People not only often blindly believe what they read, but they are also rather naive about what they see. In Pery, Ohio, they were having trouble with speeding car drivers. Because the police department was rather short-handed in this town, a life-size dummy was constructed. This dummy was dressed up in a police uniform, placed behind the steering wheel of a squad car, and driven to an area where speeding was rife. The citizens of this county, completely taken in by what they believed they saw, slowed down as soon as they detected the squad car with the dummy at the wheel.

Sometimes the desire for money makes people gullible. In 1926, in Italy, a crippled peasant named Torraca advertised that he intuitively knew which numbers would be drawn in the national lottery. In no time at all a host of people knocked at his door. "Please tell us," they begged, "some of the numbers that will be drawn." Torraca responded by saying, "My family, assisted by divine aid, found the key to the lottery. The secret was divulged to me by my father on his deathbed. But he told me I must only benefit other people and never enter the lottery myself." After this statement was printed, the crippled man received cables and letters from all over Europe, begging him for the numbers. An armed guard had to keep mobs away from his house. In the long run, of course, he sold some of the numbers, and many people pawned their possessions in order to buy tickets. When the day of the draw came, however, not one of the numbers Torraca had given out came up. And Torraca himself was missing.

Yes, it's definitely true that people are gullible, some more so than others. But there are also many people who are foolish.

Two main stories circulate as to how the earth came into being. The first is known as the "Big Bang" theory. It says that the earth be-

> *The fool has said in his heart,*
> *"There is no God."*
> *They are corrupt,*
> *They have done abominable works,*
> *There is none who does good.*
>
> *The LORD looks down from heaven upon the children of men,*
> *To see if there are any who understand, who seek God.*
> *They have all turned aside,*
> *They have together become corrupt;*
> *There is none who does good,*
> *No, not one.*

gan from a super explosion which took place some twelve to fifteen billion years ago. A very small mass of matter just happened to explode, and since that explosion things have been happening in the universe. Out of the dust particles swirling through space from the explosion, somehow the earth and other planets were formed. (If you've ever seen an explosion, such as Mount St. Helen's eruption, either on video or on TV, you'll know that there's not much of a chance that an explosion could be responsible for the orderly creation of anything, let alone our complex and beautiful world.)

The second account of how the world was made is found in the first book of the Bible, in Genesis. Here we read that the world was formed by God's command, by His spoken Word. Genesis relates that God created the world in six literal days, not in an unspecified amount of time. We can believe this magnificent truth without any qualms because this is what God tells us in a very straightforward manner in Genesis. And, after all, isn't He qualified to tell us? Wasn't He the only One there?

Have all the workers of iniquity no knowledge,
Who eat up my people as they eat bread,
And do not call on the LORD?
There they are in great fear,
For God is with the generation of the righteous.
You shame the counsel of the poor,
But the LORD is his refuge.

Oh, that the salvation of Israel would come out of Zion!
When the LORD brings back the captivity of His people,
Let Jacob rejoice and Israel be glad. Psalm 14

Both accounts of how the world was formed are mind-boggling. Neither can be proved or disproved since both deal with events that happened a long time ago, events that cannot be examined or tested. So how do you know what to believe? It's not a simple matter, you see, of mistaking a dummy for a policeman or of sending away for a bottle of fluid that you think will make your hair eternally frizzy. It's much more than that.

The Bible tells us that "the fool has said in his heart, 'There is no God'" (Ps. 14:1). To believe in God and in His Creatorship is essential for the Christian. If there is no Creator God, a God who has chosen His elect people from before the foundation of the world (Eph. 1:4), then there is also no Redeemer God.

When a person is gullible, that person is overly naive and perhaps somewhat dumb on occasion. Gullibility happens to all of us at some time or other. Being a fool, however, is a way of life and ends up, not with an embarrassed grin at a passing error, but on the left side of the Son of God (Matthew 25:33–34).

Food For Thought

1. On what do you base your actions and ideas? Do you trust your own judgment? Why/not?
2. Proverbs 28:26 says, "He who trusts in his own heart is a fool, but whoever walks wisely will be delivered." Where should you always go for advice and help?

19

Gottschalk of Saxony

In the year 805, a boy child was laid in the arms of a wealthy Saxon count. (Saxony was located in the northern part of today's Germany.) The count was thankful for this son and cradled him carefully. In an age when many children died at childbirth, or before they could toddle, his son appeared robust and healthy. Before the child was many days old, he was baptized Gottschalk.

Gottschalk was born during the time when Charles the Great, otherwise known as Charlemagne (742–814), ruled. Charlemagne had conquered Saxony and had tried to enforce Christianity on the people who lived there. For a few years, at the beginning of Charlemagne's rule, Saxons had a choice: they could either be killed or be baptized. Although this is definitely not the correct method of evangelizing, God did use Charlemagne to introduce Christianity into the Saxon area. Pagan high priests were deposed and soothsayers were imprisoned. Missionaries came and went, monasteries and churches were built, and many Christian laws were passed to improve living conditions.

By the grace of God, Gottschalk's mother and father became Christians, and they taught their small son to love God. When he

> *Therefore we also, since we are surrounded by so great a cloud of witnesses, let us lay aside every weight, and the sin which so easily ensnares us, and let us run with endurance the race that is set before us, looking unto Jesus, the author and finisher of our faith, who for the joy that was set before Him endured the cross, despising the shame, and has sat down at the right hand of the throne of God.*
>
> *For consider Him who endured such hostility from sinners against Himself, lest you become weary and discouraged in your souls. Hebrews 12:1–3*

was still very young, however, they both died and he was left a defenseless orphan. Relatives placed him in a nearby monastery. Perhaps they didn't want to be saddled with feeding and educating a growing boy, or perhaps they had their eyes on his inheritance. In any case, the monastery took Gottschalk in—as well as his land, money, and freedom.

Gottschalk grew up in the monastery, instructed in languages and Bible study by the monks who lived there. They regarded him as one of their own, and when a teenage Gottschalk, tired of monastery life, wished to leave their care, he was told he could not because his vocation was to be that of priest. Gottschalk was young. He had no father or mother to advise him. Acquiescing to the abbot of the monastery, he began studying the Bible in earnest. He grew into a lonely young man, deprived of normal family life. But what he lacked in human affection, God gave back to him in his study of Scripture. Gottschalk discovered through Bible reading, and took great comfort from the fact, that he had been chosen by God even before the foundation of the world (Eph. 1), and that nothing and no one could snatch him out of his Father's loving hand (John 10:28).

After Gottschalk took his final vows and became a monk, he was finally free to leave the monastery. He began to travel. The urge to see more than the massive stone walls of the monastery was on him. He traveled extensively through Italy, Dalmatia (today's West Yugoslavia), Pannonia (area in present Hungary and Yugoslavia), and Noricum (in today's Austria). As he walked through these regions, he preached what he had read in the Bible to everyone he met. He simply could not keep quiet. "God bestows His love freely on those he has chosen," he joyously told crowds in the villages he passed through. And the people, none of whom could read the Bible for themselves, and all of whom had been convinced by priests that the way to salvation was through giving money and by doing good works, were delighted with this message. But the priests began to hate him.

Gottschalk's teaching (look up Romans 8:28–31), which we would term "predestination," was condemned by two archbishops. They arrested Gottschalk and took him to a church council. This council, which acted like a court, found him guilty of heresy. The trial took place during the years 848–849. Refusing to deny what he said, Gottschalk was beaten almost senseless. Held by his captors, he was forced to hold a book he had written about predestination in his hands, and then physically made to throw it into a fire. His priesthood was taken away from him, and he was sentenced to life imprisonment.

Gottschalk spent the next twenty years in isolation in prison. Not one friend was permitted to see him. Although he was offered his freedom on a number of occasions if he would but promise not to teach as he had taught before, he would not compromise. He died alone in a cell at the age of sixty-three, rejected by men and denied the sacraments. But God had chosen him and no one could take that away. The child Gottschalk, the youth Gottschalk, and the man Gottschalk, had always been in God's hand and under His care. Although he died alone, humanly speaking, you can be sure he was surrounded by a cloud of witnesses in that solitary cell (Hebrews 12:1), and he was still able to write poetry such as this:

> *Jesus take care of me*
> *Into eternity*
> *And undeservedly*
> *Grant me Your mercy free*
> *So that my innermost*
> *Praises Your majesty.[1]*

Food For Thought

1. Charlemagne bullied people into being baptized and going to church. Can your parents, your teachers, or anyone you know, make you a Christian? Why/not?
2. It is said that Gottschalk could not keep quiet about what he believed God revealed to him through the Bible. He had to share it. If you don't share what you believe, if it doesn't spill over into your neighborhood, are you a real Christian? Why/not?

Note

1 Gottschalk of Germany (805–868). Translated by Christine Farenhorst from the German.

20

Chinese Anecdotes

An anecdote is a short narrative concerning a particular incident or event of an interesting or amusing nature. In general, anecdotes are pleasant to read and can illustrate certain points. In relating the following Chinese anecdotes, the points are threefold: first, that Bibles are very scarce in China; second, that it is difficult for Christians to obtain them; and third, that Chinese Christians hunger with a hunger that puts us to shame, for the Word of God. These anecdotes are not particularly amusing. They are, however, of great interest to those who belong to the universal church.

* * * * * *

Sometime during the 1990s, a farmer and his wife arrived in the huge city of Shanghai that boasts a population of some 14 million plus. Camping on the sidewalk they drew many curious glances from passers-by. Their clothes and manners gave away the fact that they were from the country and not used to the ways of the city. "Where are you from? What are you doing here camping on the

> *Then His brothers and His mother came, and standing outside they sent to Him, calling Him. And a multitude was sitting around Him; and they said to Him, "Look, Your mother and Your brothers are outside seeking You."*
>
> *But He answered them, saying, "Who is My mother, or My brothers?" And He looked around in a circle at those who sat about Him, and said, "Here are My mother and My brothers! For whoever does the will of God is My brother and My sister and mother."*
>
> *Mark 3:31–35*

sidewalk?" Questions were not long in coming from those who lived in Shanghai. The farmer was subdued and a little backward, people thought, in his answer. "I am looking for my brother." "He's looking for his brother!" People guffawed behind their hands and thought him a country bumpkin for imagining that he could find his brother just by sitting on the sidewalk. "What's your brother's name? Where does he live?" When the farmer shrugged his shoulders and answered that he didn't know, the people laughed again and walked on. The man was strange, but he had brought a smile to their drab existence, and they relished the thought of speaking to fellow workers about him.

Word got around, and a Christian couple in a nearby apartment heard of the farmer and his wife camping on the sidewalk. They also laughed a little but suddenly stopped to say to one another, "As Christians we address one another as brother and sister. Do you suppose this farmer is trying to give a message to our churches here?" Walking down to the place where the strangers were camped, the Christian man greeted them kindly. Then he said, "My father's name is Abraham; who is your father?" The farmer regarded him solemnly for a moment. Then, with tears in his eyes he responded, "My father's name is Abraham, too! You must be my brother."

The Christian couple found a Bible for the farmer and his wife. That is what they had come to Shanghai for. They left soon afterward to share that single Bible with hundreds of believers in the remote country district from which they had come.

* * * * * * *

During Chairman Mao's rule it was not uncommon for Bibles and other Christian literature to be burned in public in China while owners of the volumes were forced to watch. Bibles are thick books, and during one of these lengthy, unholy bonfires in the city of Chungking, a Christian onlooker managed to secure one page from a burning Bible. For years afterwards the underground church to which he belonged survived on this single page. A message sent by this particular underground church to the free world reads: "We have learned from this one page that Christians have to try and resemble Christ." The page that sustained their faith in those years was Matthew 16, verse 18 in particular: "And I also say to you that you are Peter, and on this rock I will build My church, and the gates of Hades shall not prevail against it." This page was printed indelibly on the hearts of these believers through the Holy Spirit.

* * * * * * *

A China news and church report of July 1994 tells the story of a group of Christians traveling through China. While they were on a train, one of the team members took out a small Bible to read for her devotions. After a few minutes a train attendant passed her and stopped to ask what she was reading. When she told him that it was the Bible, the attendant responded with: "Oh, the Bible! What does it say? Can you come to my office and tell me about it? I would really like to know more about what it says." A nearby woman, seated on one of the sleeper bunks, joined the conversation and said: "Are you Christians? I have seen a Bible and some other books on Christianity. What is it about? Can you lend me something to read about it?" When the group obligingly gave her a book, the person in the bunk above her also asked for a book. While these two were reading the material given to them, another person from the compartment came over and talked to the Christians, explaining to them that faith in the Communist Party had disappeared and that hearts were empty. "Where we go there is nothing," the young man said, "We're just wasting our lives."

* * * * * * *

In June of 1992, the State Statistics Bureau in China claimed Christians numbered 63 million. Because many believers would not take part in such a census, fearing arrest and persecution, it is believed that the actual number of believers is perhaps as high as 100 million and growing. Reports are coming in from regions where there were not thought to be any churches where thriving underground churches are flourishing. But the great shortage of Bibles remains. It is believed that there are as many as 55 million Christians without their own copy of God's Word. There are also at least 1,000 prison camps in China that hold many Christians.

In order to obtain a Bible in China, a person has to go to a state-controlled church, a church controlled by the Communist government, and fill out many forms. This provides the state with your name, address, ID number, your "unregistered" home church, and other information. People who have gone to the trouble of doing this to obtain a Bible have been detained, questioned thoroughly, and, in many cases, imprisoned. It also leads to the harassment and raiding of their "underground" church. Most people are afraid to take the risk of applying for a Bible.

A young Chinese evangelist was asked by Western missionaries what could be done to encourage the many thousands of believers in China under his pastoral care. He was silent for a long time, and then he quietly said, "Conditions for believers in China are very difficult. There are three things you can do. First, you can pray; second, you can pray; third, you can pray again."

God is building His church. The Holy Spirit moves about where He will. We should remember the words of the evangelist daily and be doubly thankful to God that He presently gives us the freedom to read His Word whenever we want.

Food For Thought

1. Do you take your Bible with you when you travel or stay overnight at a friend's house? Is it that precious to you? How often do you read it by yourself and with your family?
2. Do you believe prayer helps? Do you pray for your parents or friends when they have trouble? Do they pray for you? Would you be embarrassed to ask your Mom or Dad or friend to pray for a problem you have? Why/not?

21

Balloons

We used to play games at birthday parties in which we blew up balloons until they broke. The winner was the one whose balloon popped first. We also hung balloons from the ceiling and tied them onto chairs. They created a festive atmosphere. This was in the 1950s. Most birthday parties today still have helium-filled balloons. Florist shops also sell great big balloons with all sorts of messages inscribed on the frail, round rubber. The fact is that balloons have been around for more than two centuries. But they weren't always used for birthday parties.

Two brothers, Etienne and Joseph Montgolfier, knowing that hot air rose, launched the first known balloon in the market place of Annonay, France. Their venture attracted a lot of attention. Scores of men and women gathered around a domed structure. They laughed and pointed, quite convinced that the huge ball they were looking at would never leave the ground. They were sure Etienne and Joseph would be embarrassed and leave the market shame-faced before long. When it was whispered that the balloon would carry a heavy load of 400 pounds, there was general hilarity. But the guffawing died down as the balloon rose slowly and majestically over its bonfire of wood. Everyone ooh'd and ah'd. It rose almost 6,000 feet in the air and ten minutes after the grand take-off, slowly sank down in a field a mile and a half away. The year was 1783, just six short years away from the French Revolution.

Etienne and Joseph were excited that their invention had stayed up as long as it did. They worked at perfecting the model and later sent up a smaller, improved balloon made out of silk. They filled it with "inflammable air," or hydrogen, and moved their site from the market place in Annonay to an open square in Paris. The crowd that gathered this time was much larger than the first one had been. This second venture was even more satisfying for both the inventors and the spectators, even though the balloon met with an unfortunate end. Rising 3,000 feet into the air, it drifted some fifteen miles from Paris and scared local farming peasants half out of their wits. When it landed, they attacked it with pitchforks until it succumbed with a great last gasp.

The following century Europe went slightly "balloonatic." Jumping down from balloons with parachutes became a popular sport, even as bungee jumping was the craze of the twentieth century for a while.

Men began to travel from one location to another using the balloon. The fact that ballooning was somewhat dangerous, often leading people into the unknown, made it attractive for the adventurous-minded. They could never travel faster than the prevailing wind, and it was a very quiet sort of travel. People said that moving above the earth had a silence so profound no silence on earth could equal it. Experiments with steering and hopes of really flying resulted in a multitude of sizes and shapes of balloons.

In 1897, more than a century after the Montgolfier brothers had set ballooning in motion, Swedish explorer Andree tried to reach the North Pole in a balloon. He took two companions with him. Andree had a 170,000 cubic foot hydrogen balloon that he christened the *Eagle*. Made out of Chinese silk and said to be water resistant, it was vast and commanded respect. The initial stage of the journey went

> *"To whom then will you liken Me,*
> *Or to whom shall I be equal?" says the Holy One.*
> *Lift up your eyes on high,*
> *And see who has created these things,*
> *Who brings out their host by number;*
> *He calls them all by name,*
> *By the greatness of His might*
> *And the strength of His power;*
> *Not one is missing.*
>
> *Why do you say, O Jacob,*
> *And speak, O Israel:*
> *"My way is hidden from the LORD,*
> *And my just claim is passed over by my God"?*
> *Have you not known?*

well. Then the *Eagle* hit the Arctic mist—a mist that had no respect whatsoever for the imposing balloon. The mist froze onto the silk, and the *Eagle* was forced to land on ice. It had already traveled for three days. Andree and his friends traveled on by sled for two and a half months before they succumbed to the cold. Thirty-three years later, in 1930, their remains were discovered.

Although people today don't generally become as enthusiastic about ballooning as they do about baseball and other sports, there are still some people who indulge. There are even some who try to circumnavigate the globe. As a matter of fact, in 1999 this was accomplished. Balloons are also a tremendously useful tool for meteorologists to help forecast weather.

When all is said and done, the Montgolfier brothers were inventive and creative. Thomas Edison and Alexander Graham Bell were

Have you not heard?
The everlasting God, the LORD,
The Creator of the ends of the earth,
Neither faints nor is weary,
There is no searching of His understanding.
He gives power to the weak,
And to those who have no might He increases strength.
Even the youths shall faint and be weary,
And the young men shall utterly fall,
But those who wait on the LORD
Shall renew their strength;
They shall mount up with wings like eagles,
They shall run and not be weary,
They shall walk and not faint. Isaiah 40:25–31

also inventive and creative. But even as we admire the ingenuity of these people who invented balloons, electricity, and telephones, we have to remember this question: Who created the creators? And if we answer that question correctly, then it's only one step from using balloons, electricity, and telephones to praising the Creator.

Food For Thought

1. Today's big invention is the computer. Computers can be programmed to do an amazing number of things, but they can get

out of control and run into snags. Do you ever wonder how the wind knows where to blow? How the snow knows where to fall? How the sea knows its boundaries? Are any of these ever out of the control of their Creator? Why/not?

2. Which is easier—to praise something you have made, or to praise something God has made, such as a tree?

22

God Also Made Richard Allen An Heir

It was around the year 1770 on the plantation of Mr. Stokely in Delaware. There were fields as far as the eye could see, and there were also people as far as the eye could see, who worked the fields. These people were all black. There were men, women, children, and even babies carried about in aprons. There were people belonging to different types of families—small, large, and single. There were people of varying temperaments—even-tempered, quick-tempered, and docile. And there were tall, short, and medium-height people. All of them, however, were similar in one particular aspect: they all had souls but were not permitted to go to church.

Richard Allen belonged to one of the families who worked on the plantation. He and his parents and brothers and sisters worked hard. Although only a child, Richard could swing a double-bladed axe and build a stone wall. His talents further included that of making shoes. Mr. Stokely was indeed fortunate to have such a gifted worker on his plantation.

One evening when Richard was a teenager, a Methodist circuit preacher held a prayer meeting for the surrounding farms and

For you are all sons of God through faith in Christ Jesus. For as many of you as were baptized into Christ have put on Christ. There is neither Jew nor Greek, there is neither slave nor free, there is neither male nor female; for you are all one is Christ Jesus. And if you are Christ's, then you are Abraham's seed, and heirs according to the promise.

Now I say that the heir, as long as he is a child, does not differ at all from a slave, though he is master of all, but is under guardians and stewards until the time appointed by the father. Even so we, when we were children, were in bondage under the elements of the world. But when the fullness of time had come, God sent forth His son, born of a woman, born under the law, to redeem those who were under the law, that we might receive the adoption as sons.

And because you are sons, God has sent forth the Spirit of His Son into your hearts, crying out, "Abba, Father!" Therefore you are no longer a slave but a son, and if a son, then an heir of God through Christ. Galatians 3:26–4:7

plantations in a clearing on the Stokely farm. Richard happened to be strolling by and, hiding behind a bush, he listened to the words of this man. For most of his young life Richard had listened to the voice of his earthly master, Mr. Stokely. But when he listened to this preacher speaking from the Bible, something trembled within his heart. He was moved to believe, beyond a shadow of a doubt, that the words the preacher read were from a heavenly Master and a great desire was born within Richard to follow this heavenly Master forever. Every night of the itinerant preacher's visit, Richard hid in the bushes surrounding the clearing, soaking up the words of Holy Scripture. And God's hand, which had protected him from the time of his birth, now comforted the young boy greatly.

Not able to contain his great happiness in learning of Jesus' death for sinners and His saving grace for all who believe in Him, Richard passed on to his parents and siblings, in simple words, the Gospel message to which he had just been exposed. All who heard him speak, with the exception of his father, who felt he was too old to embrace new thoughts, believed.

After much contemplation and prayer, Richard approached his earthly master, Mr. Stokely, and asked for permission to hold Sunday worship services for all the slaves on the plantation. And God so moved the slave owner's heart that permission was given to meet in the kitchen of the great house. Not only that, Mr. Stokely was so impressed with Richard's hard work and honesty that he allowed him to buy his freedom in the year 1777.

Freedom did not make Richard any less enthusiastic about his salvation. He continued to honor the Lord in both life and work when he settled down in the city of Philadelphia. During the day he drove a wagon team, made shoes, and ran a chimney-cleaning business. But at night he preached and preached again, to all who would listen. God so blessed this work that Richard was given permission to use the white Methodist Church at five a.m. every Sunday morning to minister to those black people who were willing to come out at this early hour. In time, the black congregation to which he preached numbered eleven hundred people. This merely proved that God's Word will not return to Him empty. It will accomplish what He desires and achieve the purpose for which He sent it (Isaiah 55:11).

The white members of the Methodist church refused to let the black members worship together with them. It hurt the hearts of the new black believers. After all, did not the book of Galatians teach that "there is neither Jew nor Greek, slave nor free, male nor female, for you are all one in Christ Jesus"?

Richard Allen was moved to believe, beyond a shadow of a doubt, that the words the preacher read were from a heavenly Master and a great desire was born within him to follow this heavenly Master forever.

Richard continued to work hard and was able to buy some land elsewhere in Philadelphia. Here a church building was erected by the black members of the congregation—an independent African church. In July 1794, Richard Allen became the first African bishop in America and until the day he died, he preached the Gospel of salvation wherever God gave him opportunity.

Food For Thought

1. When the minister reads from the Apostles' Creed, what do you think the phrase "holy catholic church" means?
2. Would you feel comfortable inviting a neighbor to attend church with you? How do your neighbors know that you believe in Jesus and that this brings you much joy?

23

And Mary Went to Calabar

Mary Slessor was just a tiny slip of a girl—but her ideas were grand and as large as the world. Before she was ten years old, she regularly saved a bit of money every week (only half a penny) for the missionaries in Africa. Now, such a small amount of money may sound trivial and not worth mentioning. A half penny! What difference would a half penny make? It did make a difference to Mary, because it meant going without supper.

Mary lived in Aberdeen, Scotland, in the mid 1850s. Her father was a shoemaker who worked in a factory. He didn't earn very much money and what he did earn he drank away on ale. Often Mary would hear her father come home late at night, drunk. Often she heard her small sisters cry themselves to sleep because they were hungry, just as she was. So Mary's small gift of a half penny was a rich gift of love.

Mary lived in a slum, an area of town where the homes were very poor. There were cracks in the walls and holes in the roof, and rats lived under the floor. Mary got up at five every morning to do chores for her mother. Then at six o'clock she had to be ready and

For "whoever calls on the name of the LORD shall be saved."

How then shall they call on Him in whom they have not believed? And how shall they believe in Him of whom they have not heard? And how shall they hear without a preacher? And how shall they preach unless they are sent? As it is written:

"How beautiful are the feet of those who preach the gospel of peace,
Who bring glad tidings of good things!"
Romans 10:13–15

present in a jute factory, a factory that turned out cloth and rope. Her hours there ran until seven in the evening. But Mary did not complain. As a matter of fact, she thought herself extremely fortunate because every other day she was permitted to go to school. In this way she learned to read, and the paper she loved to read most was the Missionary Record.

Through a special gift of the Holy Spirit, Mary was filled with love for the African people she read about—people she had never seen, people who did not know about Jesus. That's why she was more than willing to be especially hungry every now and then, and give her hard-earned money away. It was her greatest dream to someday travel to Africa and tell these people about God. In the meantime, she tried teaching the children who lived with her in the slums about God. She asked them to go with her to Sunday school. Initially this turned out to be a disaster. Some of the older boys who came wrecked furniture in the classroom and threw mud at the teachers. Outside, later on, the leader of the boys had a heavy iron weight on a string. He pushed Mary against the side of a house and swung the iron weight back and forth, almost hitting her face. Mary stayed very still, looked him straight in the eye, and won the battle, and his respect, by sheer courage.

For years Mary stayed at home. Her father died, her mother was ill, and her younger brothers and sisters required care. When she was twenty-six, however, these responsibilities were fulfilled. Finally able to leave home, she began pursuit of overseas missionary work in earnest. The Foreign Missions Board sent her to a place called Calabar, situated on the West Coast of Africa.

Mary loved her new country from the moment she set foot in it. She studied the African Efik language diligently and also took long walks to get to know and understand the natives of Calabar. Her hair was cut very short. She often wore no shoes, and she laughed and sang as she climbed huge trees like a monkey. The childhood she had never really had in Scotland was presented to her on a platter. Looking at her, it was possible to mistake her for an African native. She was not a native, however. She was a missionary. Yet because of her childlike candor and enthusiasm, those she had come to speak to of her love for Christ soon grew to love her.

There were strange customs in Mary's new country, customs which she despised. One of these was cruelty to those who were weaker and smaller. A huge, painted native carrying a ten-foot whip beat a woman one day in the village center. The woman whimpered and cried. It made Mary's heart stand still with pity and she grew so angry that she ran outside with her umbrella and, without any thought for her own safety, began hitting the man. He was so surprised and dazed by her repeated blows that he dropped his whip and fell down. Afraid of her tiny, imposing stature, he ran off. Knowing God to be on her side, Mary always felt capable of administering and speaking of biblical justice.

Mary was a tiny woman, only about half the size of many of the natives with whom she worked. But she helped them when they were sick, taught them how to read, and told them about the Lord Jesus. And many believed because, through the Holy Spirit, they saw Jesus at work in her actions and they felt Jesus' love in her words.

Mary was convinced God had given her the job of looking after the bodies and souls of this particular African people. She traveled to where they needed her most—deeply into the jungle. She taught women how to cook properly, how to keep clean, and how to sew. She even ventured into cannibal territory, and here, too, people converted and God's Word was spread.

In 1915, crippled by arthritis and a constant fever, Mary died. She died among the Calabar people where she had been allowed to build hospitals, schools, and churches. Hundreds of natives wailed and tore their clothes at the funeral. They had been able to learn much from Mary Slessor, a tiny missionary, who, through the Holy Spirit, had been able to touch their hearts with God's love.

≋

Food For Thought

1. Would you be willing to give up one meal every week and give that money to, for example, the Middle Eastern Reformed Fellowship (a ministry to the Arab people)? What are you presently doing for missions?

2. Was it incorrect for Mary, as a woman, to become involved in missionary work? (Read 1 Cor. 14:34 but keep in mind that Mary helped establish churches which were not there yet, doing much practical work in the process.)

24

Of Chicks and Men

When I was eleven years old or thereabouts, I found a baby robin chirping away helplessly in the lilac bushes straddling our driveway. Peeping for all it was worth, it was scrawny and wide-eyed. Seeing no mother robin hovering nearby, I picked the baby chick up very carefully, cradling it in the palm of my right hand. A shoebox served as its nest that night as I tried, at intervals, to feed the starving chick. But it would not have anything to do with the dead flies I had collected in a little pile, neither would it take the water and milk I offered through an eyedropper. All my ministrations were of no avail. The next morning the little shoebox had become a little bird coffin.

It takes much skill and know-how to hand-feed and raise baby birds. The type of food baby birds require and the temperatures at which they must be kept are important factors. Because the importation of tropical birds destined for North America and Europe is being banned by many countries, there is an increase in artificially incubated, hand-reared birds. Birds are popular pets.

Bird hatching and raising has been around for centuries. It may surprise you to know that some 4,000 years ago, the Egyptians were already incubating eggs artificially to increase their poultry output. And they had some amazing techniques! Certain people made hatching birds a family business and their "methods" of producing live and healthy chicks were kept secret, passed down from father to son.

The center for artificial hatching was in the village of Berme. Here eggs were collected from all over Egypt and brought back for incubation. The village had some 386 ovens. These were used six months of the year and eight broods could be hatched during this time period. Some 30,000 chicks were hatched from each brood making an approximate total of 92,604,000 chicks per breeding season.

Historical records have revealed some of the "secret" methods that the Egyptians used as they handled the fragile, oval shells. Egg temperatures were tested by holding an egg against the corner of the eye. (Try feeling the corner of your eye and you'll be amazed at how sensitive this spot is to hot and cold.) Breeders used eggs less than a week old and held them up against the sunlight to check embryo age by the size of the air sac.

The ovens in Berme were large, each consisting of a number of smaller chambers. These chambers were all connected by small openings that could be closed off. There were openings for air, light, and heat. The top chambers of the ovens were filled with manure and straw. The straw and manure burned slowly, providing heat for the chambers below. Eggs were continually moved from chamber to chamber as heat distribution was irregular. Too much heat was dangerous and too little heat was likewise fatal. It took know-how about when to switch chambers and when to add straw to the top chambers to incubate healthy chicks. Once the chicks were hatched, they were removed from the ovens to a different rearing area in the village.

* * * * * * *

There is, of course, no real substitute for a genuine mother hen, whose plumage covers chicks with a steady warmth, caring more

> *Remember the days of old,*
> *Consider the years of many generations.*
> *Ask your father, and he will show you;*
> *Your elders, and they will tell you:*
> *When the Most High divided their inheritance to the nations,*
> *When He separated the sons of Adam,*
> *He set the boundaries of the peoples*
> *According to the number of the children of Israel.*
> *For the LORD's portion is His people,*
> *Jacob is the place of His inheritance.*

correctly than any surrogate. Artificial is and remains artificial. There is something very touching and beautiful in seeing mother and father birds feed their young.

The Lord compares Himself to a bird in Deuteronomy 32. Certain birds, you see, will sacrifice their own lives to protect their chicks. They will stand against powerful enemies to shelter little ones. The Lord is like that. He spreads His protection, like the wings of an eagle, over His children, warming them, raising them, catching them when they fall, and feeding them. Indeed, He has done so even at the cost of His own Son.

Food For Thought

1. The Egyptians had access to some amazing techniques with regard to raising chicks. They did not praise the Creator God for

> *He found him in a desert land*
> *And in the wasteland, a howling wilderness;*
> *He encircled him, He instructed him,*
> *He kept him as the apple of His eye.*
> *As an eagle stirs up its nest,*
> *Hovers over its young,*
> *Spreading out its wings, taking them up,*
> *Carrying them on its wings. Deuteronomy 32:7–11*

the wonder of creation, however. How is modern man like the ancient Egyptian in this respect?

2. Do you believe that the Lord knows exactly what sort of environment His children need? Do you believe he will protect and shelter His people? (Read Isaiah 31:5.) In light of the obvious answer, why is it not correct to grumble and complain about your home, your parents, your schooling, etc.?

25

A Matter of Hearing

On a clear day in September in the year 1816, Dr. René Laennec was out walking in the hospital gardens of Paris. Lost in thought, he wandered off the neatly laid out path and tripped over a log in front of his feet. Stumbling awkwardly, he almost fell. The motion snapped him out of his reverie. To his surprise he found himself in a wooded area where three boys were playing a game. Rather tired from all his walking and his thinking, Dr. Laennec sat down on the forest floor and in curiosity watched the children. They were playing with a piece of lumber—a long piece of wood. One boy had a pin in his hand. "I'm going to scratch the board at this end," he cried. "See if you can hear it at the other end." The two boys at the other end were ready, one standing and the other bent down with his ear to the wood. "Can you hear me?" the first boy yelled. "No," said the youngster who was standing and "Yes" cried the other with his ear down on the board, "I can hear you as plain as day." They took turns scratching and listening as Dr. Laennec watched in fascination.

It was providential that Dr. Laennec stumbled across the boys playing in a secluded part of the hospital gardens, and it led to a dis-

A wise man will hear and increase learning,
And a man of understanding will attain wise counsel,
To understand a proverb and an enigma,
The words of the wise and their riddles.
The fear of the LORD is the beginning of knowledge,
But fools despise wisdom and instruction.
Proverbs 1:5–7

covery that would save many lives. The game gave Dr. Laennec much food for thought, and after a good number of hours of thinking he put the boys' game into practice—into medical practice. He rolled several sheets of paper into a tight roll. Pressing one end of this cylinder against a patient's chest, he put his ear against the other end of the tube. And then, even though his ear was quite a distance away from the patient's chest, he could hear the heartbeat quite plainly.

For months, Dr. Laennec experimented with the idea. He built all sorts of tubes with various kinds of wood. He named his new invention a "baton," but it was later renamed the stethoscope. It proved to be a wonderful aid in the prevention of disease because it enabled doctors to detect heart and lung problems in early stages.

It is important to listen to and think about things we encounter every day. God has given us ears with which to hear and minds with which to think.

* * * * * * * *

Rev. Adoniram Judson Sr. was a middle-aged man when he married Abigail Brown. They had three children, and Rev. Judson was very proud of all three of them. He was especially proud, however, of his oldest son, Adoniram Jr. Little Adoniram was a quick child, who, by the time he was three, was already able to read many verses from the Bible. His father told him many times that surely God would use him—that surely God had a plan for his agile mind, and that he would grow up to become someone great and special in God's eyes.

In the year 1804, when Adoniram was sixteen and ready to enter college, an examination showed that he already knew much of the material which was being taught. Because of this, Adoniram was permitted to skip the first year of college. There was no question at all that God had endowed Adoniram with a perceiving mind, a thinking mind. But was Adoniram also able to listen, to listen and understand what God had in mind for his life?

Adoniram made friends in college. One of his best friends was a boy named Jacob Eames. Jacob, although he was a pleasant fellow, was a deist. He thought that the Bible was no more important than any other book; he thought God was far removed from mankind; and he believed that heaven and hell were figments of the imagination. Adoniram often heard Jacob speak of his beliefs, and Adoniram was taken in by his friend's words. When Jacob spoke of wealth and power, arguing that these two mattered the most in life, Adoniram agreed. Deep down inside he knew Jacob was wrong, but Adoniram stopped up the ears of his heart and grieved the Spirit of God within him.

After he finished college, Adoniram left home and moved to New York in search of fame and fortune. But like the Prodigal Son, fame and fortune eluded him in the end, and one day he found himself without food and with very little money. Destitute and unsure, Adoniram began to travel back home. He stopped overnight at a wayside inn and asked for a cheap room. There was only one left, the innkeeper informed him, and it was next to a young man who was very ill, perhaps dying. But Adoniram, all too happy to have accommodations, did not care.

That night he had trouble sleeping. The thought of death hovered over him like a blanket and invaded his thoughts. Was the young man in the room next to him prepared to die? Was he himself prepared to die? Adoniram became afraid. His childhood training, words of Holy Scripture, scrambled about in his mind. What if the Bible had been right after all about heaven and hell?

After a sleepless night, the faint light of dawn shone through the window. Birds began to chirp outside, and all the warmth and joy of living filled Adoniram's mind. He laughed at his fears and got up. How could he have spent the night thinking somber and dismal thoughts? He dressed and walked down the stairs to the front desk. Paying his bill, he casually asked the innkeeper how the ill man was. "He is dead." The answer came quickly and without any emotion on the innkeeper's part. "Dead?" For a moment the night's fears crept back into Adoniram's being. Then he shook himself. The sun was shining. What was the matter with him? He spoke to reassure himself. "That's too bad. What was the fellow's name?" The answer came to him from God, although the words were uttered by the innkeeper. "The man's name was Jacob Eames."

Adoniram rode home much affected. He could not help but think deeply as his horse alternately walked and cantered, and he knew it was no coincidence that he had spent this particular night at this particular inn. God had confronted him with death. God had warned him. And Adoniram listened and changed his life.

In 1812 Adoniram went to India as a missionary, and from there he traveled on to Burma. He was the first missionary hailing from North America. His faith in Christ was strong, and God permitted him to translate the Bible into Burmese.

* * * * * * *

Nothing happens by chance. The invention of the stethoscope did not happen by chance, and it saved many lives. The translation of the Bible into Burmese did not happen by chance either, and it saved many souls.

Food For Thought

1. God determines all the steps of a man. Proverbs 16:9 says, "A man's heart plans his way, but the LORD directs his steps." When you think about what happened to you today, how do you see God's purpose in it—even in the little things?
2. Jesus said, "He who has ears to hear let him hear." What did He mean?

26

Remember Your Leaders (1)

Truly China is a separate country, remote from other nations. The huge, Himalaya Mountains cut her off from India. Her north and west borders feature desert. There is also a wall—a great, stone wall, twenty to thirty feet high and fifteen to twenty feet thick—stretching 1,400 miles between China and Mongolia. As such, it seems almost impossible for the Chinese people to be able to receive news about the Lord Jesus Christ. Yet God says in His Word that every knee will bow before Him.

At the end of the thirteenth century, Marco Polo, the explorer, traveled into China. He was amazed at all the things he saw, and he began to love the Chinese people. He also obtained an audience with the Kublai Khan, the great ruler of China. And when Marco returned to his native Italy, he carried with him a letter from the Khan to the pope asking for one hundred learned monks to teach the Chinese people about Christianity. God surely guided the Khan's hand and heart to request such a thing. Chinese knees would also bow before Him. But the request for missionaries went almost unheeded by the western world. Two monks went, but they were fainthearted and returned to their

Look to Me, and be saved,
All you ends of the earth!
For I am God, and there is no other.
I have sworn by Myself;
The word has gone out of My mouth in righteousness,
And shall not return,
That to Me every knee shall bow,
Every tongue shall take an oath.

homeland without spreading the Gospel. The door to China, opened just a crack by the Lord, shut again. China stayed isolated.

In the 1850s, trading posts were established (with the Chinese Emperor's permission) by France and Britain. Through this the door to China opened once again to missionaries. One of these missionaries was a man named Hudson Taylor. When Hudson Taylor first arrived in China, a Chinese man asked him a heart-rending question. "How long have you had the Gospel of Christ in your country?" "Some hundreds of years," Hudson replied. "What? Hundred of years! My father was looking for the Truth. He died without knowing about it! Why did you not come sooner?"

Two missionaries who came to China in the twentieth century were John and Betty Stam.

John and Betty met at the Moody Bible Institute. They both felt a strong calling by the Lord to serve in China. They were certainly not drawn to the mission field by money or lifestyle. Conditions were bad in China in the 1930s. The communists were fast taking over the country and things were not peaceful. Towns were often looted by soldiers, and many citizens were either murdered or jailed. So why did John and Betty feel compelled to leave the relative safety and security of their homes and country?

Betty wrote her reason down. She wrote: "I want to invest this

> *He shall say,*
> *"Surely in the LORD I have righteousness and strength.*
> *To Him men shall come,*
> *And all shall be ashamed*
> *Who are incensed against Him.*
> *In the LORD all the descendants of Israel*
> *Shall be justified, and shall glory." Isaiah 45:22–25*

one life of mine as wisely as possible, in the place that yields richest profits to the world and me. This may not be in China; it may be in India or Africa, or our own squalid slums in New York. But, wherever it is, I want it to be God's choice for me and not my own. There must be no self-interest at all."

Betty was a year ahead of John in school and was accepted for China mission work eight months before he was. She could recall much of the Chinese language, as she had been raised in China by missionary parents. It was a great joy to both John and Betty when John was also accepted to serve the Lord in China.

In October 1933 John and Betty were married. It was a beautiful wedding. Two children of the King, a prince and a princess in Christ, committing their lives to the Lord and each other.

Food For Thought

1. Should you only speak to the people in your church about your faith? Will we be held responsible for all the people we meet

whom we did not speak to about our Lord and Savior, Jesus Christ? (Read Ezek. 3:18–21 before you discuss your answer.)

2. How important is it to marry within God's royal family, that is to say, does God require us to marry a Christian man or woman? (If you are unsure, check out 2 Cor. 6:14.)

27

Remember Your Leaders (2)

Those first months in China meant much language study for both John and Betty. They lived with another missionary couple. Many fine, new Chinese Christians encouraged them with love and by example. It was dangerous to be a Christian in China. Yet many new Chinese Christians fearlessly preached and followed God's law.

In 1934, John and Betty had a little baby—Helen Priscilla. They were very happy and anxious to move to their own mission station in the town of Tsingteh. Although there was talk of communist troops advancing into the area where the Stams would live, most people were convinced that these communist troops posed no immediate threat.

John and Betty arrived in Tsingteh at the end of November in 1934. It was no easy move. They had to walk 200 miles, carrying bedding, clothes, books, and some food. Two men came along to help them. When they stopped to rest, they often sold many Gospels and used the opportunity to speak to people about God who had sent his Son, Jesus Christ, into the world to save sinners. And many people listened to the friendly white couple with the tiny baby.

How beautiful upon the mountains
Are the feet of him who brings good news,
Who proclaims peace,
Who brings glad tidings of good things,
Who proclaims salvation,
Who says to Zion,
"Your God reigns!"
Your watchmen shall lift up their voices,
With their voices they shall sing together;
For they shall see eye to eye

Tsingteh lay in a valley amid towering mountains. Many of its houses were crumbling, old palaces. The landscape beyond the city magnified God's name—clear streams and soaring peaks. John, Betty, and baby Helen moved into an ancient Chinese house, taking the place of another Christian couple who had already lived there for a year. God had allowed this other couple to bear fruit in preaching and teaching, and so it was that there were a number of dedicated Chinese Christians willing and ready to help the Stams.

December 6 appeared a normal day. In the early morning hours Betty bathed baby Helen and played with her. John was busy writing some letters. It was during these early hours that Tsingteh was captured by the communists. The takeover happened so quickly and unexpectedly that there was no chance of escape. There was panic and shooting in the streets. John and Betty knelt down and prayed with the two servants. They relied totally on God.

It did not take the soldiers long to come to the house to arrest John. They bound him and took him away. Shortly afterwards they

When the LORD brings back Zion.
Break forth into joy, sing together,
You waste places of Jerusalem!
For the LORD has comforted His people,
He has redeemed Jerusalem.
The LORD has made bare His holy arm
In the eyes of all the nations;
And all the ends of the earth shall see
The salvation of our God. Isaiah 52:7–10

also came for Betty and the baby. But John and Betty thanked God that they could be together during the next few hours. They felt close to the Lord and prayed earnestly. John was then released for a short time during which he was able to secure more food and clothing for the baby. He told the frightened servants huddled together at his home, "Don't be afraid. God is on His throne. These little things are immaterial—our Heavenly Father knows all about them."

Somehow John also managed to write a letter to the China Inland Mission, the Mission which had sent them out. He wrote: "Dear Brethren, my wife, baby, and myself are today in the hands of the communists, in the city of Tsingteh. Their demand is twenty thousand dollars for our release. All our possessions and supplies are in their hands, but we praise God for peace in our hearts and a meal tonight. God grant you wisdom in what you do, and us fortitude, courage, and peace of heart. He is able—and a wonderful Friend in such a time. Things happened so quickly this morning. They were in the city just a few hours after the ever-persistent rumors really became alarming, so that we could not prepare to

When the guards came, they left the sleeping bag on the bed. (Thirty hours later another Christian found the baby there, alive and well, and smuggled her away.)

leave in time. We were just too late. The Lord bless and guide you, and as for us, may God be glorified whether by life or by death. In Him, John C. Stam."

Meanwhile, anarchy reigned in Tsingteh and the surrounding area. Many people, given no chance to defend themselves, were killed for no apparent reason. John and Betty were led out of the city the next day, along with a group of other people, toward the neighboring village of Miaosheo. A man recognized the Stams and whispered, "Where are you going?" John answered, "We do not know where they are going, but we are going to heaven." That night they were taken to a room, and John was bound to the frame of a bed. Betty was allowed to remain untied so that she could tend baby Helen.

At dawn, on December 8, 1934, Betty zipped baby Helen up inside a warm sleeping bag and put her on the bed. When the guards came, they bound both John and Betty with ropes. They left the sleeping bag on the bed. (Thirty hours later another Christian found the baby there, alive and well, and smuggled her away.) John and Betty were marched to a hill outside of the town. In the face of obvious death, they showed no fear and many villagers were awed by their calmness. Surely their God was mighty. John was commanded to kneel, and with one stroke of a sword his head was hewn off. Betty also knelt, and her soul entered heaven but a step behind John's.

That John and Betty Stam, twenty-seven and twenty-eight years young, should die so early in their service for the Lord is difficult to understand. But that they were a seed of the Chinese church and a shining example to us, is a sure thing. And that they are now rejoicing with their Father in heaven, is clear as crystal. "Remember your leaders, who spoke the word of God to you. Consider the outcome of their way of life and imitate their faith" (Hebrews 13:7 NIV).

Food For Thought

1. If you, or your parents, died today, would your lifestyle be worth imitating? Why/not?
2. Do you know many people whose "feet are beautiful," that is to say, people who are eager to bring the Gospel of Christ to others? Who are they? Are your feet beautiful? Why/not?

28

Comfort, Comfort

In 1551, a pastor by the name of Jean Jocry traveled back to his native France from Switzerland. He had studied in Geneva for a number of years and was carrying Protestant books in his backpack. As he walked the country roads, he was accompanied by a young boy. The lad was his apprentice who studied under him as he preached in the towns they passed. Jocry had hardly crossed the Swiss border, however, when he was arrested and his backpack searched by the French Roman Catholic Church authorities. Carrying Protestant literature was forbidden in France. Both Jocry and the boy were consequently jailed and condemned to death at the stake. Jocry appealed the sentence to a higher court at Toulouse. He and the boy were taken there. Fearlessly the pastor confessed his faith, proving what he said by quoting numerous Scripture passages. The boy pledged the same faith as his master, but because of his youth and inexperience, was unable to defend himself as ably as Jocry. Their sentence at Toulouse remained the same as the previous sentence: death at the stake.

On the day they were to burn, many priests and monks came to persuade the two "heretics" to recant. When they would not, Jocry

> *"Comfort, yes, comfort My people!"*
> *Says your God.*
> *"Speak comfort to Jerusalem, and cry out to her,*
> *That her warfare is ended,*
> *That her iniquity is pardoned;*
> *For she has received from the LORD's hand*
> *Double for all her sins." Isaiah 40:1–2*

and his young friend were tied to a crossbeam above a woodpile. The priests and monks surrounded the young boy and bothered him so by their words that he began to weep. Jocry, tied up close by him, said, "Why do you weep, little brother? Don't you know that we are about to go to our most High and Gracious God, and that presently we shall be free from all this sorrow?" The boy answered, "I wept because you were not with me." "There is no time for weeping now," Jocry replied gently. "Rather, let us praise the Lord." They began to sing a psalm together, and the boy was encouraged and comforted.

When the fire began to singe Jocry's body, his concern was not for himself but for his young charge. Pulling himself up against the stake, he spoke words of comfort and encouragement to the lad. When he perceived that the boy had died, he also readily gave himself over to the flames. Soon his head fell and his spirit was received by his Lord.

* * * * * * *

During the sixteenth century, many priests could not even read—let alone explain the Bible—to the people in their congregation. Most were acquainted only with "divine bookkeeping"—the prices for administering baptism, marriage, and the last rites. People began to resent the fat clergy who walked around forever wanting money but never giving comfort in either life or death. When the Protestant Reformers began their preaching, the people listened to the message of the Gospel with amazement and joy. The words that were preached offered salvation and the salvation was free. "For by grace you have been saved through faith, and that not of yourselves; it is the gift of God" (Eph. 2:8).

One of the European rulers at this time was Frederick III. Frederick III felt compassion for the needs of the people in his Palatinate, an area he ruled in southwest Germany. Frederick was a Protestant. He saw that many in Europe were persecuted for their Protestant faith. He also knew that these believers did not have ready access to Bibles. There were no Gideon Bible Societies, neither were there second-hand bookstores where you could buy a Bible cheaply. Besides that, very few people could read. Praying for guidance, Frederick abolished the festivals of Mary and the saints in his own Palatinate. Altars, organs, ornate baptismal fonts, and images disappeared from his churches. Appointing Protestants as teachers and preachers, Frederick III gave two steadfast men a mandate to put together a booklet. "Write down, in simple words," he said, "what the Bible teaches."

Kaspar Olevianus, the court preacher, and Zacharius Ursinus, a professor at the Heidelberg University, both loved the Lord very much. They prayerfully accepted the task Frederick gave them and wrote down biblical teaching in a unique question-and-answer way. People who could not possibly memorize and know the whole Bible by heart could learn much about the basic doctrines of the Bible through the questions and answers in the booklet Ursinus and Olevianus had written.

Many of those persecuted were not as well acquainted with the Bible as pastor Jocry had been. As pastor Jocry's apprentice had been in need of words of encouragement, these people also needed encouragement. They needed it as they were dying in dark, dirty dungeons with iron chains chafing their legs; they needed it dying under torture; and they needed it dying at the stake. The first question Ursinus and Olevianus wrote began with comfort. "What is your only comfort in life and death?" The answer was resoundingly beautiful. It begins like this:

> That I am not my own, but belong—body and soul, in life and death—to my faithful Savior, Jesus Christ.

It goes on to say:

> He (God) watches over me in such a way that not a hair can fall from my head without the will of my Father in heaven.

Ursinus and Olevianus made up a total of 129 questions and answers about the main doctrines of the Bible. Every answer was proven by Bible texts so that no one could say they were wrong. The Heidelberg Catechism (which is what the question and answer booklet became known as) became a little booklet of comfort for people who desperately needed it.

Food for Thought

1. If the Bible were ever taken away from you, would you have some of it committed to memory? What passages do you know?
2. Certain foods are known as "comfort" foods, such as chicken noodle soup taken when people have a cold, or a hot cup of tea when people are tired after a hard day at work. Is the Bible "comfort" reading at your house every day? When do you read it and how much time do you take to talk about God's comfort with your family?

29

Life Sentence

The oldest castle in England is not exactly the dream vacation resort where many people would choose to spend their holidays. Since its erection by William the Conqueror in 1078, it has been a great many things—a royal court, an armory, a jewel house, a zoo, a royal mint, and also, a state prison. Most people know this castle by its last designation, the Tower of London.

The Tower of London was definitely not a place where the average Englishman would spend a few days of fun and leisure. All the buildings comprising the castle were made with walls at least eight feet thick. Foreboding drawbridges, guards, and slits in these walls, permitting the pouring of molten lead or boiling water on enemies, made people just a trifle uneasy when they registered for a visit. Besides this, the moat surrounding the castle, full of mud, slime, and sewage, was very unattractive. It was also an established, but grim fact, that once you were a prisoner in the Tower of London, it was probably for life.

Over the years there were a number of prisoners who tried to escape from the forbidding Tower. One of these was a man named

> *Then Jesus returned in the power of the Spirit to Galilee, and news of Him went out through all the surrounding region. And He taught in their synagogues, being glorified by all.*
>
> *So he came to Nazareth, where He had been brought up. And as His custom was, He went into the synagogue on the Sabbath day, and stood up to read. And He was handed the book of the prophet Isaiah. And when He had opened the book, He found the place where it was written:*
>
> *"The Spirit of the LORD is upon me,*
> *Because He has anointed Me*

Edmond Nevill. In 1580, accused of being in a plot to kill Elizabeth the First, he was imprisoned in the Tower of London. There was no trial.

Edmond Nevill, being a skilled and inventive man, found a way over the months of ensuing imprisonment to pick up bits of metal here and there. Fashioning himself a file of sorts, he worked at his prison bars until he could manage to crawl out. He scaled the impressive wall, swam the filthy moat, and disappeared from sight. The morning after his escape found him six miles away from London. But that, unhappily for Mr. Nevill, was the end of his taste of freedom. Soldiers caught up with him, and under heavy escort he was taken back to the Tower. Secured by leg irons this time, he was fastened to a wooden pillar in his cell.

Six long years passed. By 1590, Edmond Nevill was classified as a model prisoner and given the privilege of visitors and daily walks outside. He managed to secure another file from bits of metal and repeated his first trick. He was now imprisoned on a higher level

> *To preach the gospel to the poor;*
> *He has sent Me to heal the brokenhearted,*
> *To preach deliverance to the captives*
> *And recovery of sight to the blind,*
> *To set at liberty those who are oppressed,*
> *To preach the acceptable year of the LORD."*
>
> *Then He closed the book, and gave it back to the attendant and sat down. And the eyes of all who were in the synagogue were fixed on Him. And He began to say to them, "Today this Scripture is fulfilled in your hearing."*
> *Luke 4:14–21*

than the one on which he had previously been imprisoned, but, with the help of visitors, had obtained a rope. One dark night, after he had fastened the rope to a secure point within the cell, he climbed out of his cell window once more and slid down toward the moat. Unfortunately, the rope was too short. Precariously dangling, he decided to chance it and drop into the moat. The splash he consequently created, however, brought many soldiers running onto the wharf. Scrambling out of the water quickly, Edmond pretended to be one of them, shouting, "Stop that man!" and "There he goes!" But one of the soldiers, upon touching him, discovered that he was wet. The game was over once more. It was back to the Tower prison for Edmond Nevill.

Closely confined for a third time, with his limbs in iron manacles, Edmond's mind was free, active, and very much bent on escaping. When, after a few months, the chains were removed, he tried something new. It was now 1596. Every time the jailer came in with his food, Edmond would sit motionless by the window, not even twitching a muscle. The warden concluded that this quiet and subdued Edmond had finally learned his lesson.

When visitors were permitted once again, Edmond secured spare clothes from them. He deftly assembled these into a dummy figure, stuffing it with straw from his mattress. It resembled himself. When it was almost time for the warden to bring his food, Edmond placed the dummy by the window and positioned himself behind the door. As the warden placed the food by the silent figure, Edmond snuck out, ran down the stairs and into the courtyard. But in the full sunlight a woman stopped him. "Who are you?" Even as she spoke, the warden came out and stared at him. "Not you again?" And back up to his cell Edmond went.

You will be happy to hear, at this depressing juncture, that two years later, in 1598, Edmond Nevill was released and still enjoyed some forty-two years of life with his wife and children.

* * * * * * *

Oscar Wilde wrote:

> . . . *every prison that men build*
> *Is built with bricks of shame,*
> *And bound with bars lest Christ should see*
> *How men their brothers maim.*

There is no doubt about the fact that it is distressing to be a prisoner. To be tied up and not to have freedom of movement must be extremely frustrating.

And yet the truth is that every single person in the whole world is a prisoner. Everyone—young, old, short, tall, intelligent, and short-tempered—everyone is a prisoner, not of the Tower of London or of the State Penitentiary, but of the State of Sin (Gal. 3:22). To be released we do not need files, ropes, or disguises; to be released we need the Messiah. Luke 4 tells us about this freedom. And yet again, the strange part about this freedom is that it is, in effect, a life sentence—a life sentence of service to the Messiah.

Food For Thought

1. Can you think of any particular habit that holds you or your family captive? (e.g. smoking, drinking, attending movies which are not suitable) How can you be made free from such bad habits?

2. Why do you think that some people might prefer to be prisoners of the State of Sin, rather than accept freedom in Christ? What kind of work does freedom in Christ entail?

30

The Day of Slaughter

Ozymandias, Trajan, Septimius Severus, and Decius—what do these tongue twisters have in common besides being difficult to pronounce? Although it's true that these names all ring a trifle unusual in our society of Johns, Dicks, and Harrys, they do have more in common than being difficult to pronounce. Add Nero, Domitian, and Diocletian to the list, and perhaps your memory will be jolted. The men who bore these names, with the exception of one, were all Roman emperors. Besides being Roman emperors, however, these men also had something else that bound them together.

Persecution in the early Christian church was not as constant as we generally think it was. There were periods when the church thrived in relative tranquility. (As a point of interest, it has been estimated that more people have been martyred for Christ in the past fifty years than in the entire first 300 years of the church's existence. Martyrdom goes on today. In Uganda alone, under the cruel leadership of Idi Amin, some 400,000 Christians died, disappeared, or fled from that country between 1971 and 1976. Besides the obvious countries of Russia and China, Christians have been martyred in

> *Come now, you rich, weep and howl for your miseries that are coming upon you! Your riches are corrupted, and your garments are moth-eaten. Your gold and silver are corroded, and their corrosion will be a witness against you and will eat your flesh like fire. You have heaped up treasure in the last days. Indeed the wages of the laborers who mowed your fields, which you kept back by fraud, cry out; and the cries of the reapers have reached the ears of the Lord of Sabaoth.*
>
> *You have lived on the earth in pleasure and luxury; you have fattened your hearts as in a day of slaughter. James 5:1–5*

some 180 other countries during this century.) From A.D. 30 to 311 only about twelve Roman emperors, out of the fifty-four who ruled during that time, persecuted Christians. The emperors mentioned above were some of the most evil rulers.

Being able to wield power can do strange things to people. There is the danger that people begin to feel that they are ultimately in control of their own destiny and the destinies of others. The emperor Domitian (81–96), for example, was skilled in warfare, besides being a wonderful architect and administrator. But these gifts obviously went to his head because he was the first emperor to call himself "God the Lord" and "Lord of the earth." Domitian killed those who would not worship him, and the devil smiled at his inability to deal with wealth and power.

The emperor Trajan (98–117) was likewise a skilled ruler. He won wars, conquered land, and was famous for building the Aqua Trajana, an aqueduct that served Rome. He also drew up the architectural plans for a gigantic forum. Demanding that all people living in his empire worship only his gods, Trajan took his power out of bounds and many Christians were killed.

The emperor Septimius Severus (193–211) was a magnificent soldier, a man of great physique, someone others looked up to. His charisma and strong personality gave him great power, but he misused this power by dwelling on his own ideas. He forced people into worshiping the sun-god Mithras—a god popular with soldiers. He forbad conversions to Christianity and again overstepped the authority God had given him. Many Christians were killed.

Much the same can be related about the other nine Roman emperors who consciously persecuted God's people. They never acknowledged that their power came from God, and in their foolishness they thought they could follow their own agenda.

The English poet, Percy Byssche Shelley (1792–1822), wrote a poem that has to do with the transience, the passing, of earthly power that man thinks he will have forever. His poem was about a man named Ozymandias of Egypt, a mighty ruler and an incredible builder. But in spite of all the power that Ozymandias had and in spite of all the great things he built, he died. The only thing that remained behind to remind people he had been alive was a crumbling pedestal in a desert with words written on it. In the first two lines, the poet Shelley has Ozymandias brag before he dies. He is conceited and proud of his own works. In the last three lines, Shelley mocks the power that Ozymandias thought would be his forever.

"My name is Ozymandias, king of kings:
Look on my works, ye Mighty, and despair!"
Nothing beside remains. Round the decay
Of that colossal wreck, boundless and bare,
The lone and level sands stretch far away.

In the long run, the abilities and power we have in life have to be viewed as a gift of God. They also have to be viewed as either honoring God or dishonoring Him. No one will live forever or be saved by "the multitude of an army" or "by great strength" (Ps. 33:16). Human works and efforts are only a matter of years. They do not last. It is well to take the words of Matthew 6:19–21 to heart, dealing with treasures we heap up.

In the year 320, during the reign of the emperor Licinius, all Christians were once more ordered to recant their faith or die. Forty soldiers of the Twelfth Legion, stationed in Sebaste in Armenia, refused to do so. They were stripped of their clothes and forced onto a frozen lake. As a lure to get them to recant, fires were built on the shore and warm baths were prepared for those willing to deny God. Only one of the forty gave in. But one of the guarding soldiers on the shore, moved by the example of the Christians, took his place. Within twenty-four hours the forty soldiers were dead. Although it is very likely that none of these soldiers built palaces or constructed coliseums, they leave behind a much greater legacy than Ozymandias's crumbling pillar. That legacy is Christ, and He endures forever and ever.

Food For Thought

1. If you were to die tomorrow, what would your parents, your friends, and your neighbors remember you for?
2. How can you build a legacy in the Lord?

31

The Girl From Hope End

It was a huge house. It had domes, minarets, and stained glass windows. It boasted a music room with a great organ and a library with shelf upon shelf of books. It even had a name—a very happy name—the name of Hope End.

Every evening a service was held in the library. Mr. Edward Barrett, the owner of the house, would read a piece from the Bible, and then everyone knelt down as he prayed with them. The whole household, from stable-boy to head-cook to Mrs. Barrett and the children, attended. One evening Mr. Barrett called back his eldest after prayer had been said. Elizabeth was not surprised. Her father often called her back, and then they would have a talk. "Elizabeth," he said on this particular night in 1813, "I've decided to let you study Greek." Now this would not be so strange if Elizabeth had been a bit older. But she was only seven. And even stranger was the fact that she was as happy as a lark with her father's announcement. And when she was eight, yes, Elizabeth was able to read Greek.

Elizabeth Barrett was born in Coxhoe Hall, Northumberland,

My heart is overflowing with a good theme;
I recite my composition concerning the King;
My tongue is the pen of a ready writer. Psalm 45:1

England, in the year 1806. Her father was a wealthy but very strict man. He expected his children to obey him without any questions whatsoever. There were eleven children in all, of which Elizabeth was the firstborn.

The Barretts were a close family and loved writing little verses to one another for birthdays or other occasions. Elizabeth seemed particularly good at this. When she was but five, one of her poems was rewarded by her father with a ten shilling note in an envelope which read "to the poet laureate of Hope End."

Elizabeth was not a bookworm. She did not just sit down on the couch and read all the time. She loved riding, climbing trees, and running around in the garden with all her brothers and sisters. She was also very aware that many of the families living on her father's estate of Hope End were a beggarly, ragged bunch who could not read or write and who were often very hungry. Her father once took her to London, and they passed Newgate Prison. Elizabeth saw women and children behind iron, grilled bars begging food from passers-by. She also saw a party of women, chained together, with small children clutching at their skirts, herded down to convict ships. Elizabeth thought hard about the fact that the world was made up of more situations than her own easy life at Hope End.

When Elizabeth became a little older, she wrote stories and poems, selling them to her father and mother, using the money to buy some of the neighborhood children clothes and toys. She also wrote a poem entitled, "The Cry of the Children." It began:

Do ye hear the children weeping, O my brothers,
Ere the sorrow comes with years?
They are leaning their young heads against their mothers,
And that cannot stop their tears.

It was a very long poem, and when it was read by the people of England, it made many reflect about injustices committed and about the poverty to which many English children were accustomed.

Elizabeth had a gift, you see, and that gift was poetry, and it came, as all gifts do, from God. Once, during holidays, when she was only eight years old, she wrote a poem about the ocean. It began:

The German Ocean rolls upon my sight
O wat'ry world of brilliant light;
The proud rocks overhang the sea,
The sounds afford a walk for me
When there, the mighty hand of God
I saw in every step I trod.

That's pretty good for an eight-year-old, don't you think?

Elizabeth Barrett Browning (Browning was her married name) became a famous poetess. Whether she knew it or not, God used her pen mightily a number of times to glorify His name. (We do know that later on in life, unfortunately, Elizabeth became interested in spiritualism.*) Nevertheless, God permitted her pen to let people see economic injustice; to describe how beautiful He had made the world; and to speak tenderly of human love.

---

* Spiritualism—the belief that the dead survive as spirits that can communicate with the living, especially with the help of a third party called a medium. Such communications were expressly forbidden by God. See Leviticus 20:6, 27.

Food For Thought

1. You may not come from an estate called Hope End, but if your trust is in the Lord Jesus Christ, you are certainly going to one. Should your heart, therefore, be stirred by a "noble theme," and should your tongue be moved to write "verses for the King"? How?

2. Elizabeth Barrett was not born with a pen in her mouth. She studied hard as a child. She perfected the gift God had given her by practicing and polishing phrases and sentences. How does God hold us responsible for hours wasted, for not fully honing the talent(s) he has given us? What happened to the man in Luke 19 who did not increase his talents?

32

Let Him Who Boasts

A small baby boy was born in France in the year of our Lord 1510. The baby's parents were poor and unable to provide an education for the child. When young Ambroise, for that was the child's name, was a little older, he severely regretted this, for he thirsted for knowledge and greatly desired to become a doctor. But he accepted with cheerful countenance the fact that he was poor, as well as the fact that it did not please God to favor him with a physician's schooling.

His parents, however, with persistent perseverance, were able to apprentice their son to a barber-surgeon. The truth is that at this particular time of history, barbers' functions were not limited to shaving and cutting hair. They also performed minor surgery and traveled about the countryside cutting off infected limbs, extracting teeth, and offering services of this sort to anyone who trusted in their expertise. Their instruments consisted of a set of knives, and a great many of their patients unfortunately bled to death. To this day the symbol of a barber is a pole striped with red (for blood) and white (for bandages).

> *Thus says the* LORD:
>
> *"Let not the wise man glory in his wisdom,*
> *Let not the mighty man glory in his might,*
> *Nor let the rich man glory in his riches;*
> *But let him who glories glory in this,*
> *That he understands and knows Me,*
> *That I am the* LORD, *exercising lovingkindness, judgment,*
> *and righteousness in the earth.*
> *For in these I delight," says the* LORD. *Jeremiah 9:23–24*

Ambroise Paré loved his apprenticeship with the barber-surgeon. He was fascinated by "operations." Gentle by nature, he was saddened by the pain patients had to bear and resolved to spend his life learning how to ease that pain. He still had no money to attend medical school, nor could he speak Latin or Greek, the languages medical textbooks were written in. But, hungry for knowledge and desiring to serve, Ambroise obtained a job in a hospital in Paris—a hospital situated on the river Seine. He spent three years there.

Now hospitals during Ambroise Paré's time did not in any way resemble our modern hospitals. Actually, they were not even called hospitals. Run by religious orders, they were referred to as institutions of charity. Frightening places, they consisted of huge beds with three or four patients crowded together in each one, sometimes with feet and heads alternating. Usually men and women were not kept separate. Contagion was unheard of, except in cases of the plague. No one had any idea that there was a connection between dirt and disease, and sheets were often covered with pus and filth. Lice were abundant, and if you were not severely ill before you came into such a place of charity, it was likely you would become severely ill. The

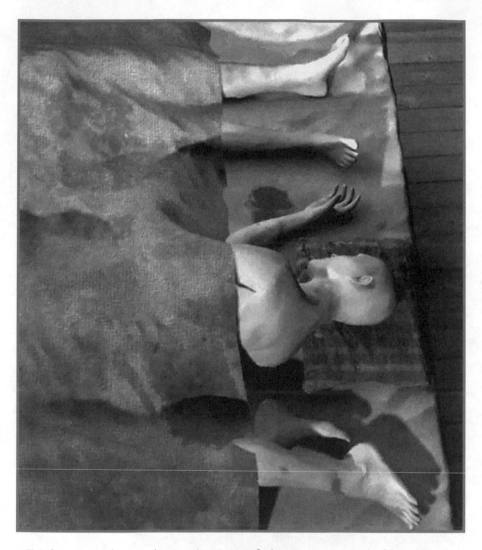

Frightening places, the institutions of charity consisted of huge beds with three or four patients crowded together in each one, sometimes with feet and heads alternating.

building itself was damp and cold, and the bathroom consisted of a hole in the floor at one end of the ward. The stench was horrible!

Ambroise Paré learned much in this institution, merely by observation and practice. In 1536, when he was twenty-six, war broke out between France and the Holy Roman Empire. Ambroise was taken on as the surgeon to a French marshal in the army. His duties were that of shaving the marshal each day and caring for him if he was wounded. Meanwhile, he was also given permission to treat other soldiers who were hurt.

Some of the standard weapons used on the battlefield at this time were rifles and pistols. Because these were used at close range, most wounds were accompanied by powder burns (believed to be poisonous). The treatment for such burns was the pouring of boiling oil around the wound's edge. This was excruciatingly painful and did not help in the least. Although Ambroise first used this treatment, he ran out of oil one day. Not wanting to leave the wounds untreated, he made up his own dressing out of egg yolk, oil of roses, and turpentine. To his surprise his patients fared much better than the ones who had boiling oil poured on their burns.

Although Ambroise never went back to the boiling oil remedy after this, he did, consequently, mix up some rather strange potions. The ingredients for one, for example, included newborn puppies and earthworms. Despite his somewhat odd concoctions, Ambroise Paré was a man much beloved by the soldiers. It was a custom at that time to cut the throats of those who were badly wounded to put them out of their misery, but Ambroise forbade this and worked compassionately with every man who was hurt. When someone improved and became better, he never wanted personal praise but would always say, "I dressed the wound but God healed you."

Ambroise served in two wars and was able, through God's grace, to save many men from death. It was common practice to amputate shattered limbs on the battlefield. This was anything but pleasant since there were no anesthetics. The only way known to prevent bleeding after amputation was by cauterization, which meant applying red-hot irons to the amputated stump or dipping the stump in a pot of boiling oil. Ambroise Paré had read of a different technique. It was called ligation, the tying off of blood vessels with thread. It was a successful technique and much less painful than cauterization. Again, when men became better because of the skill he had acquired at this technique, Ambroise refused to take the credit. "I dressed the wound," he repeated again and again, "but God healed you."

Later in life Ambroise was given the title of Master Surgeon, though he never did earn a medical degree, even becoming surgeon to the French king. Living to a ripe old age, he practiced medicine until he died at the age of eighty.

Ambroise Paré was not free from superstitions or from Roman Catholic thoughts. Nevertheless, we can learn something from him. He had a sense of humility and love enabling him to praise God in all his work. The Bible says, "Let him who boasts boast in the Lord" (2 Cor. 10:17 NIV). Ambroise Paré did.

Food For Thought

1. When you are praised abundantly for something you did, do you find it difficult to turn that praise into a compliment for God? Should we do so? Why/not?

2. Ambroise Paré had to overcome public opinion that human life could be done away with if, humanly speaking, nothing more could be done. Do doctors today face a similar problem? If so, what is that problem?

33

It Rarely Happens

Throughout the Middle Ages there were many battles between the English and the French. The year of our Lord 1346 was another such time. The English had the upper hand and were besieging the French city of Calais.

The city of Calais was in a strategic position. Located on the sea coast, it was the French city closest to England. It was also the most difficult city to capture. The walls were exceedingly thick. Its towers were high, and the people upon the embattlements* defending the city were so sheltered that they could hardly be injured. A moat flowed around the walls which could only be crossed by a draw-bridge behind which a portcullis† was always ready to drop on un-wanted intruders.

The English King, Edward III, desperately wanted control of the fortress of Calais. Control of Calais, so close to the Straits of Dover, might win him the French crown. But how could he conquer such

---

* A low wall with open spaces for shooting, built on top of a castle wall, tower, or fort.
† A large, heavy iron grating with spikes beneath it.

> *For when we were still without strength, in due time Christ died for the ungodly. For scarcely for a righteous man will one die; yet perhaps for a good man someone would even dare to die. But God demonstrates His own love toward us, in that while we were still sinners, Christ died for us. Romans 5:6–8*

an impregnable place? Fill the moat with earth and logs and put ladders against the wall? Use battering rams? Have mangonels* hurl stones? Use moving towers? Edward's knights tried all these tricks of war to no avail. The besieged people of Calais put mattresses over the edge of the wall to receive the blows of the battering rams; they threw stones and other heavy objects on the people below; and they toppled ladders as soon as these touched the sides of the wall. Indeed, the people of Calais caused their English attackers much harm.

King Edward was nonplussed. And then he did a very clever thing—he did nothing. When the French citizens of Calais looked down from their turrets one morning, they saw a peaceful army encamped outside their walls. A herald did ride up to the gates calling upon Calais to surrender to King Edward, but when the city refused to do so, the herald merely rode back to the camp. There was no fuss, no bother with weapons anymore. There were no more preparations for fighting. Tents were pitched. Small wooden huts were built, and these were thatched with straw. These tents and huts were arranged in rows like streets, and after a while a pattern of living became apparent. Each Saturday local farmers and butchers would come to sell their wares. The seashore brought English merchants to the strange town, and they brought cloth and weapons. It finally

---

* Old military slingshot-type apparatus for hurling heavy stones and other missiles.

dawned upon the people of Calais that Edward could live there permanently, starving them all to death. Their only hope was that the King of France, Philippe, would gather an army together to rescue them.

The Governor of Calais was worried. Food became scarce. To save on supplies, he caused all the poor of the city to be sent outside of the gates. Perhaps this was merciful as these would have been certain to starve first. This group of 1,700 people, weeping as they went, was so pitiful a sight that King Edward ordered they should rest at his camp city, eat, and be given a small sum of money before they went on their way.

King Philippe did try to send supplies to his loyal Calais subjects. But he found it extremely difficult to get food into a city surrounded by English soldiers. The small amount of bread and meat smuggled in were not nearly enough to sustain the city. The people within reached a breaking point. A whole year had passed. It was obvious to all of them that no further help would be forthcoming.

The Governor of Calais now suggested in a parley that Edward be content with taking the city while letting the inhabitants go in peace. King Edward would not agree. "I will receive the city of Calais," he said, "only on the condition that I can kill whom I please and imprison whom I please." The brave answer sent back was, "These conditions are too hard for us. We are but a small number of knights and squires, who have loyally served our King, and who have suffered much." King Edward then relented somewhat. He said that he would pardon the city and its citizens on the condition that six of the chief citizens would die for all of Calais. They were to carry the keys of Calais to him, coming out of the city on bare feet, wearing no hats, having halters on their necks.

Upon hearing King Edward's decision, the Governor caused a great bell to be rung. The ringing brought all the people together in the city square. The Governor wept as he related to the people the terms that King Edward had given. Huddled together, the crowd resembled little more than scarecrows. A thin, tall man stepped out of the multitude of wails. "It would be a pity," he said, "if all of our citizens were to die of starvation with free food so nearby. To give them food would surely please God. I have such faith and trust in the grace of God that I myself will be the first of the six to go out to die for my fellow citizens." Such was his example, that five other men followed his lead without hesitation.

Barefoot, bareheaded, with halters around their necks, the humbled men were led into the presence of King Edward. Giving him the keys of Calais, one of them said, "We yield ourselves to your absolute will and pleasure, in order to save the remaining inhabitants of the town. We appeal to you to have pity on us."

King Edward, however, remained stern and commanded that the group of six should be beheaded. His nobles, softened by the sight of these courageous men, entreated him to have mercy. But he would not listen. The headsman was already approaching when Queen Philippa, tears running down her face, knelt down in front of her husband. Her pleas moved him to compassion, and he allowed her to do what she pleased with these men. And she was pleased to feed and dismiss each one with a gift of six gold coins.

The Bible tells us in Romans 5:7 that it is extremely unusual for someone to be willing to die for someone else. Certainly the men of Calais were an exception. They chose to give their lives for their fellow citizens.

A man named William Hendriksen wrote a poem on Romans 5. Part of that poem, a stanza on verses 7 and 8, reads:

> *It rarely happens that a man*
> *For someone who is righteous can*
> *Be found to die. But though it's rare*
> *Yet for a good man one might dare*

To give his life. But God above
Showed his incomparable love
In that, while we were sinners still
Christ died for us. Such was His will.[1]

Food For Thought

1. Proverbs 25:21–22 tells us, "If your enemy is hungry, give him bread to eat; and if he is thirsty, give him water to drink; for so you will heap coals of fire on his head, and the LORD will reward you." If someone has been unkind to you, has cheated you, has gossiped about you, what is the proper response?
2. Some people say they love licorice; others say they love skating; still others say they love holidays. When it speaks about God's love in Romans 5:8, is it a different kind of love? Why do you have to know that you are a sinner in order to understand this love?

Note

1   From the *New Testament Commentary on Romans* by William Hendriksen.

34

Then The Lord Called Samuel (1)

Once upon a time there was a prince and his name was Kaboo. You might laugh. Kaboo is not a common name. But the truth is that there really was a Prince Kaboo born around the year 1872. He was born into the Kru tribe, which lived deep in the jungle of Western Africa. And God had mercy on this little baby and set him apart.

Being a prince of one of the tribes along the Ivory Coast of Africa was not as easy as you might think. There were none of the luxuries of Buckingham Palace, but there was much warfare. Kaboo's father, although the king of a tribe, was neither rich nor powerful. He usually lost his battles and had to pay heavy war fines. In one of his battles he gave away his son, Prince Kaboo, as a pawn—as insurance that he would pay his fine. This was bad news for Kaboo. Pawns were often beaten and starved. Twice Kaboo was given away and twice he was bought back by his father.

Kaboo was fifteen years old when his father gave him away for the third time. This third time his father was unable to buy him back. Mercilessly Kaboo was beaten every day with a thorny, poisonous

Then Saul, still breathing threats and murder against the disciples of the Lord, went to the high priest and asked letters from him to the synagogues of Damascus, so that if he found any who were of the Way, whether men or women, he might bring them bound to Jerusalem.

As he journeyed he came near Damascus, and suddenly a light shone around him from heaven. Then he fell to the ground, and heard a voice saying to him, "Saul, Saul, why are you persecuting Me?"

And he said, "Who are You, Lord?"

Then the Lord said, "I am Jesus, whom you are persecuting. It is hard for you to kick against the goads."

So he, trembling and astonished, said, "Lord, what do You want me to do?"

Then the Lord said to him, "Arise and go into the city, and you will be told what you must do." Acts 9:1–6

vine. It tore his flesh and made him ill. When Kaboo was unable to stand up any longer, a cross-tree was erected, and he was thrown over it. Preparations were made to kill him.

Wracked with pain, Kaboo, young as he was, welcomed the thought of death. But as he lay half-conscious across the tree, suddenly a great flash of light surrounded him. He heard a voice, but saw no one. The voice told him to rise and to flee. He obeyed the voice. Not having eaten for some time, he was weak with hunger and weary with pain, but somehow this voice filled him with restored strength.

Kaboo, who had never heard of God, could feel power coursing through him. He had no idea in which direction he should run. If he ran back to his family, they would be attacked again. But the light guided him. It led him through the night, past poisonous puffadders, crocodiles, and leopards, and kept him safe from the numerous cannibal tribes who lived in the jungle.

After many nights of following the light, Kaboo came to a plantation near Monrovia, a city in Liberia. He obtained a job which included sleeping quarters, food, and some clothes. With curiosity he saw a fellow worker pray and was easily persuaded to go with him to a church meeting. Providentially, the missionary spoke of Paul's conversion, when he fell to the ground and the light from heaven flashed around him. Kaboo stood up and shouted aloud in excitement when he heard these things. "I have seen this light! Yes, I have seen this light!"

The missionary, amazed at Kaboo's story, ministered to the teenager, even as Ananias had ministered to Paul. Kaboo loved the Bible stories and, moved by the Holy Spirit, grew to have faith in the Lord Jesus. As he grew, he was moved by a desire to go back to his tribe and tell his people what he had learned. But he also felt that the fear and hatred he harbored in his heart would not permit it. He cried out to God and God heard his pleas. The hatred gradually left Kaboo and love and peace took its place. Not too many weeks later, Kaboo was baptized and renamed Samuel Morris.

Food For Thought

1. Does having a childlike faith mean that you have to be a child? What does it mean?
2. Because it is difficult to witness to other people if you have fear, hatred, or anger in your heart, it should be a priority to be filled with love. How is this done? Can you give any practical examples?

35

Then The Lord Called Samuel (2)

Prince Kaboo, or Sammy as he was now known, still needed to learn much before he could become a missionary to his own people. He was especially fascinated by the Holy Spirit Who, he knew, had taken away the bitterness and anger in his own heart. He was told that there were schools in America that taught much about the Bible, and, desiring above all to be taught, he found his way to the sea coast. Approaching the captain of a small vessel, he asked, with childlike faith, to be taken on board.

Hired on as a crew member, Sammy spent the next six months aboard the ship. Ill-equipped to work the deck, he was made cabin boy to the captain. The captain was an alcoholic. In one of his drunken fits he kicked Sammy unconscious. When Sammy came to, he did not reproach the captain but resumed his work cheerfully, praying fervently. Despite himself, the captain was moved. As with the captain, so Sammy was with the crew. His unselfish love in nursing the sick, in fearlessly stepping between men who were fighting, gradually changed the atmosphere on the ship. The captain repented of his alcoholism and consequently forbade the use of rum

> *But the fruit of the Spirit is love, joy, peace, longsuffering, kindness, goodness, faithfulness, gentleness, self-control. Against such there is no law. And those who are Christ's have crucified the flesh with its passions and desires. If we live in the Spirit, let us also walk in the Spirit. Let us not become conceited, provoking one another, envying one another. Galatians 5:22–26*

on board. Quarrels ceased and Sammy sang for the men on the deck in the cool of the evenings. When they finally reached New York, the crew took up a collection and bought Sammy some clothes.

Sammy had been told by the missionaries in Liberia that a man by the name of Stephen Merritt in New York was very knowledgeable about the Holy Spirit. So directly after walking off the gangplank, Sammy set out to find him. A passer-by directed him to Merritt's office, and Sammy ran to a man just locking the door. "I am Samuel Morris," he said, "I have just come from Africa to talk with you about the Holy Ghost." Understandably the man, who turned out to be Merritt, was surprised. But after speaking with the boy, he took Sammy home and put him up for the night. The next day he took Sammy with him to a funeral. They drove down to the church in a coach, and Merritt took the opportunity to show Sammy some of the sights of New York. After a while, however, Sammy knelt down on the floor of the coach and prayed: "Father, I have been months coming to see Stephen Merritt so that I could talk to him about the Holy Spirit. Now that I am here, he shows me the harbor, the churches, the banks, and other buildings, but does not say a word about this Spirit I am so anxious to know more about. Fill him with Thyself so that he will not think, or talk, or write, or preach about anything but Thee and the Holy Spirit." The prayer filled Merritt, and others present, with awe and love for the small, thin, black boy. Merritt's sermon was powerful during the funeral and many were moved to know the Lord.

After having Sammy stay at his home for a period of time, Merritt sent a letter to Taylor University in Indiana, asking that the young teenager be admitted. The Young People Society in his church also raised a sum of money to provide him with books, clothes, and transportation. Sammy was about eighteen years old at this time, and his hunger for learning more about his heavenly Father had not abated.

Sammy loved university. A special tutor was provided for him because his knowledge was limited. He proved to be a very diligent student and was able to retain all the information he was fed. When he received visitors in his small room, he would ask them to read the Bible to him. His tuition was paid through a Samuel Morris Faith fund. Sammy never touched a penny of this fund for personal use. He lived on the barest necessities and wanted the rest of "God's money," as he called it, to be used for people more worthy than himself.

Sammy yearned with great yearning for the time when he would be able to return to his own country. Once he hurt his hand. The outer skin was broken so that the hand showed up white. He put ink on the skin, afraid that it might remain white, explaining as he did so that it might be a disgrace and hindrance to the Gospel on his return to his people.

Sammy grew in wisdom and knowledge. God permitted him to lead many students to Christ with his simple faith and trust and his strong assurance of the Holy Spirit's power. However, the early years in Africa had weakened his body. The cold winters in America were hard on him. The winter of 1892–93 was especially severe. Sammy caught a bad cold that lingered and lingered and finally made him bed-ridden. He prayed for sound health and was very disappointed when God did not heal him of his malady. But he received peace through continual prayer and said to his visitors. "I am so happy. I have seen the angels. They are coming for me soon. The light my Father in heaven sent to save me when I was hanging helpless on that cross in Africa was for a purpose. I was saved for a purpose. Now I have fulfilled that purpose. My work here on earth is finished. The work in Africa is Christ's work. He will choose others who will do a better job than I could have done."

Sammy died before he was twenty-one. After his death several other young men volunteered to go to Africa in Sammy's place. Taylor University became a training ground for missionary work. Sammy had indeed been saved for a purpose.

Food For Thought

1. Where do you go to seek out the purpose for your life? Which friends do you go to for advice?
2. Why was Sammy content to die? Would you be content to die if God should so choose? Why/not?

36

Child of Music—Child of God

Every year, during the Easter season, there's a good chance that people will be singing those songs that commemorate the death and resurrection of our Lord Jesus Christ. Some of these songs are joyful and full of abundant notes. One such song is "Christ the Lord is Risen Today." Other songs are mournful and filled with trembling compassion and emotion, such as "O Sacred Head Now Wounded." The music for "O Sacred Head Now Wounded" was written by a man called Johann Sebastian Bach. He wrote much music, and he loved the Lord Jesus, his Savior, very much.

Johann Sebastian Bach was born in 1685 in a little town in Germany called Eisenach. His father, Ambrosius Bach, rocked Johann in his arms when he was a tiny baby and often sang to him. Notes cradled about him and fed him even as his mother's milk fed him. His father also probably taught little Johann to play the violin before he could read. Throughout his early years Johann went to sleep each night to the sound of singing. His parents' friends often came to play their musical instruments in the evening, and they filled the air with notes.

Praise the LORD!

Praise God in His sanctuary;
Praise Him in His mighty firmament!

Praise Him for His mighty acts;
Praise Him according to His excellent greatness!

Praise Him with the sound of the trumpet;
Praise Him with the lute and harp!
Praise Him with the timbrel and dance;
Praise Him with stringed instruments and flutes!
Praise Him with loud cymbals;
Praise Him with high sounding cymbals!

Let everything that has breath praise the LORD.

Praise the LORD! Psalm 150

Music was nothing new to the Bach family. For nearly 200 years members of their family had played the organ in churches around Germany. They had also written much music. It was as if God had put notes into their veins, instead of blood.

When small Johann was eight, he went to school and learned the four Rs—reading, writing, 'rithmetic, and religion. He enjoyed learning and was always at the top of his class. But he still loved it best when his father sat down with him and said, "Johann, I have a new song for you to learn." When Johann was almost ten, his carefree childhood ended abruptly. His mother, who had often read the Bible to him, and whom he loved dearly, died. Within seven months his father married again. Just when Johann was getting used to this change, his father also died. In the space of less than a year, Johann had become an orphan. Suddenly, when he crawled into bed at night, there was no longer any music; there were only tears.

One of Johann's older brothers, who had just gotten married himself, took the lad in. It was a kind act, but it was extremely difficult for a ten-year-old boy, used to warmth, laughter, and a lot of hugs, to suddenly become a boarder, to suddenly lose his parental home.

Music comforted Johann. God, his heavenly Father, had given it to him; Ambrosius, his earthly father, had encouraged him; and Elisabeth, his mother, had taught him to be thankful for it. The music was always with Johann. It ran through him like a brook. The word "Bach" means brook, and Johann's music, like his name, always flowed.

Johann began writing the music down. He rejoiced in the notes running gracefully across the pages. But before he began composing, before he put down any notes, he always wrote "Jesu, Juva" at the top of the paper. It meant "Jesus, help me." And when he finished composing, he wrote the initials S.D.G.—"Soli Deo Gloria"—at the bottom of the page. Translated it means, "To God alone the glory."

It's a wonderful thing when we try to please God in what we do. Johann was very aware of that. He wrote some very special music. As a matter of fact, it's some of the most beautiful music in the world today. The name of this music is "The St. Matthew's Passion." It was the custom of Johann's church in Germany to set the story of Jesus' last days to music. The words were taken directly from the Bible and were sung by a narrator called the "Evangelist." Choirs sang the choruses. There were other characters that sang, too: the High Priest, Pilate, Judas, Peter, and even Jesus Himself.

Before Johann began composing, he always wrote "Jesu, Juva" ("Jesus, help me.") When he finished composing, he wrote S.D.G.—"Soli Deo Gloria" ("To God alone the glory")—at the bottom of the page.

Listening to "The St. Matthew's Passion" you can hear the song "O Sacred Head Now Wounded" a number of times. You'll also be able to feel, through the music and the songs, how much Bach loved his Lord Jesus Christ. And, even more importantly, through this music you can hear and feel with a Christian sense how much Jesus loved those for whom He died.

Food For Thought

1. From reading Psalm 150, we know that it is important to God to be praised with music. How often do you and your family and friends praise God with the sound of the trumpet, harp, and lyre, or any other musical instrument? If you do not, is this wrong?

2. Is it a good habit to begin putting "Jesus, help me" at the top of projects and "To God alone the glory," as a signature? Why/not?

37

On the Palms of God's Hands

A pick-up truck was driving down a rather steep hill. It held a family of six: a father, a mother, and four young children. They were happy, singing and laughing as the truck drove downhill. Suddenly one of the back wheels came off. The truck edged sharply over to the shoulder of the road and further. It was out of control and within seconds had rolled sixty feet down the cliff side of the road. All four children, thrown clear of the truck, were unconscious. The mother was hurt rather badly. She had broken both her legs and her pelvis, but she was conscious. Overcoming the pain, she pulled herself out of the truck and instinctively crawled, on her belly, over toward her children. Her husband was not hurt as badly as she was, but he was unable to stop his wife from leaving the truck. She seemed impelled by an inner desire to be with and to help each individual child.[1]

Although this is a true story, we don't know what happened to each member in this particular family. But we do know this for a fact—God has instilled in mothers a wonderful instinct for their children. Even though many mothers today deny this gift,

> *Can a woman forget her nursing child,*
> *And not have compassion on the son of her womb?*
> *Surely they may forget,*
> *Yet I will not forget you.*
> *See, I have inscribed you on the palms of My hands;*
> *Your walls are continually before Me. Isaiah 49:15–16*

it is, nevertheless, a God-given instinct that the following story also illustrates.

＊ ＊ ＊ ＊ ＊ ＊ ＊

It was a hot day. The windows were open wide in the Scottish church. The minister's resonant voice easily carried outside onto the lawn beside the building. "A long time ago," the minister said, "my father led expeditions in these highlands. On one of his trips, the group he was with heard a small child wail. As they searched the area for the source of the crying, they found a dead woman with a small boy in her arms. She had frozen to death. A poor widow, she had been on her way back to her birth village. Carrying all she owned, she had trudged many weary miles with the little one in her arms. Overtaken by hunger and cold, her last thoughts had been that she must shelter this child. She lay down in such a way that her body protected him from the elements and the warmth she still possessed passed on to her child. Because of her love, the boy was still alive when he was found by my father's expedition party."

The minister paused. He looked at his congregation for a moment before he continued. "If you think that the love of this mother was wonderful, than I will speak to you now of a much greater love. That love is the love of our God and Father who sent His only Son to die for those He loved and chose before the foundation of the world."

After the service, a young man who had been listening to his words outside by the church window, approached the pastor. "The story you told," he said, "was my story. I was the child found by the wayside and the mother who died was my mother. She loved me so much that she was willing to die for me." He stopped and looked directly at the minister. "But now," he continued, "I would like to hear more of this Father."

* * * * * * *

Our Father in heaven is a wonderful Father. In His everlasting plan, a plan made even before the foundation of the world (Eph. 1:4–5), He determined how His children would be saved. The Bible tells us His love surpasses even that of a good, earthly mother. "Can a woman forget her nursing child and not have compassion on the son of her womb? Surely they may forget, yet I will not forget you. See, I have inscribed you on the palms of my hands" (Isaiah 49:15–16b).

Some speak of Mother's Day and others of Father's Day, but surely Good Friday—the day the palms were engraved—is the best day of all.

Food For Thought

1. Is your faith merely head knowledge? How are your hands involved in your Christianity?

2. What do you think the phrase "engraved on the palms of My hands" means?

Note

1 Paraphrased from "Where's Dad" by Weldon Hardenbrook, pg. 387 in *Recovering Biblical Manhood and Womanhood.*

38

Eligius

Deep within the bowels of a dark, Germanic forest, a small boy stood with his mother and other members of his tribe. He listened to the chanting of a priest mingled with the raucous cawing of a passing crow. The forest was cool and dismal, and the child was afraid. A cow had just been sacrificed, and its glistening intestines were spread out on stones and moss. A second priest was reading the intestines, muttering to himself about what their design and color meant for the tribe. The small boy clasped his mother's hand a little tighter when an owl hooted in the distance. A bad sign surely. Perhaps it was an evil spirit hovering over the area. A mouse rustled the blades of grass near his feet, and the boy whimpered. "Shhh," his mother whispered softly and squeezed his hand. It was important that they remain perfectly quiet so that the priest could read the future with as much hope as possible.

It was A.D. 585 and the small boy, Eligius, was five years old. Up to this point his life had been fraught with constant fears. Danger seemed to threaten everywhere. He was taught that evil spirits roamed about freely and that the souls of the dead could harm him.

Sorcerers and witches, as well as powerful priests, exacted food and other things from his family. And when Eligius thought about death, he shuddered, even as he saw his father and mother shudder. Death, the priests taught, meant blackness and no hope.

By the grace of God young Eligius and his tribe met a number of men from Ireland who had come to settle in the wilderness and to live with the Germanic tribes. The leader of these men was a sturdy Irishman named Columban. Eligius saw these men work alongside his parents. Not afraid of hard labor, they cleared wastelands, and as they cleared the land they talked. It was unlike anything Eligius had ever heard before. "There is only one God," Columban said, "and He has created the world so that we might live in it and praise Him." Eligius heard the creation story, the story of the fall into sin, and the story of redemption, and, again by the grace of God, he believed and was not afraid any longer.

When Eligius was a teenager, he became apprenticed to a gold-smith and learned his trade well. He learned it so well, as a matter of fact, that he became known throughout the Frankish* country for his skill. The king of the Franks, Dagobert, offered him a position at court, and Eligius accepted. He expertly minted gold coins for the king and became a wealthy man. His time of poverty and fear seemed long ago. Eligius, however, did not forget his childhood. He often walked the countryside and gave money to the poor and sick, speaking to them at the same time about the love that God had shown to the world. Eligius did more than that. He also visited the foreign slave market and regularly purchased slaves off the dock. Sometimes he bought as many as fifty slaves in one day. He took these slaves home and treated them well, giving them clean clothes and plenty of food. Then he spoke to them about God. After a cer-

---

* A Frank was a member of a group of ancient German people dwelling in the re-gion of the Rhine River. His country was known as the Frankish kingdom.

> *What does it profit, my brethren, if someone says he has*
> *faith but does not have works? Can faith save him? If a*
> *brother or sister is naked and destitute of daily food, and one*
> *of you says to them, "Depart in peace, be warmed and filled,"*
> *but you do not give them the things which are needed for the*
> *body, what does it profit? Thus also faith by itself, if it does*
> *not have works, is dead. James 2:14–17*

tain period of time he freed them and let them go back to their own country, hoping these men would, in turn, speak to their countrymen about God. Many of these men did not, but some did.

When Eligius became older, he felt a tremendous desire within himself to become a missionary and to speak of God's love to the Frisian people. (Frisia was the area that we now know as the Netherlands.) The king, although loath to see his expert goldsmith leave, finally gave Eligius permission to become a missionary. Eligius worked in Frisia until his death. Often he was mocked and reviled but he was also permitted to build churches. He died in the year 658, and his very last words were of God's love. A portion of one of his sermons, now more than thirteen hundred years old, still speaks to us today and reads: "He is a good Christian who washes the feet of those who seek shelter at his house, showing as much love to them as he would to his beloved parents; who gives alms to the poor to the best of his ability; who visits the church faithfully and lays his gifts on God's altar; who does not enjoy his first fruits until he has given a portion of them to God; who does not use counterfeit money or dishonest scales; who does not practice usury; who lives a chaste life and encourages his sons and neighbors to likewise live chaste lives in the fear of the Lord; who, prior to the holy ceremonies which take place in the church, together with his wife, practices chastity in order to approach God's altar with a clear conscience; and who, finally, memorizes the Apostles' Creed and the Lord's Prayer and teaches them to his sons and daughters. Without any doubt, such a man is a Christian." Eligius, like James, upheld the principle that faith without works is dead. As such, the words of his sermon, although spoken so many centuries ago, serve to encourage us today in Christian living.

Food For Thought

1. Genuine faith, real faith, will produce actions of love. How is faith evident in your life? In your parents' lives?

2. James 2:26 says, "For as the body without the spirit is dead, so faith without works is dead also." If you have no actions or deeds, why should you be worried about having faith?

39

Mary Peck's Heart

Mary Peck was born in the early 1700s in Rehoboth, Massachusetts. A healthy, robust child, not afraid to work, she helped her innkeeper father run his business. Cooking, washing, and cleaning were second nature to her, and her forceful, strong character made her, as she grew up, quite influential in her town.

When Mary was twenty-five, she married a man by the name of John Butterworth. He was a house wright (a craftsman at building houses) and a good carpenter. People did not refer to Mary as Mrs. Butterworth though. But they referred to John as "Mary Peck's husband."

John was not a poor man by any means. He owned his own house plus some land, and had two men working for him. He was a good provider and Mary was blessed as his wife. However, Mary was not satisfied. She longed for more money and material things, even though she already had much. Mary attended church every Sunday, but she had apparently never heard a sermon on 1 Timothy 6:10 which says, "For the love of money is a root of all kinds of evil, for which some have strayed from the faith in their greediness, and pierced themselves through with many sorrows."

> *Do not lay up for yourselves treasures on earth, where moth and rust destroy and where thieves break in and steal; but lay up for yourselves treasures in heaven, where neither moth nor rust destroys and where thieves do not break in and steal. For where your treasure is, there your heart will be also.*
>
> *The lamp of the body is the eye. If therefore your eye is good, your whole body will be full of light. But if your eye is bad, your whole body will be full of darkness. If therefore the light that is in you is darkness, how great is that darkness!*
>
> *No one can serve two masters; for either he will hate the one and love the other, or else he will be loyal to the one and despise the other. You cannot serve God and mammon.*
> *Matthew 6:19–24*

There was not too much money circulating in the colonies at this time. In order to provide money and to finance military expeditions, the governments of Massachusetts, Connecticut, and Rhode Island issued paper currency, money known as "bills of credit." These bills were merely crude pieces of paper, and when Mary Peck held one in her hand, thoughts of large sums of money began to drift through her head.

Many people had tried their hand at counterfeiting the bills of credit, but most of them were caught. Spurred on by greed, Mary invented a method that left no incriminating evidence. Her method was fairly simple. She lay a piece of starched muslin on a bill of credit. Then she heated up her iron and ran it over both. The muslin received the impression of the bill. She then placed the muslin over a piece of blank paper, heated up the iron again and ran it over the blank paper and the muslin. The impression was now on the blank paper. With a fine, quill pen Mary traced the impression carefully. Then she threw the muslin into her fireplace.

Not satisfied with counterfeiting only a few bills, Mary organized family members into helping her with her dishonesty, including the two men who worked for her husband. She also had seven passers—people who bought the counterfeit bills from Mary at half price and passed them out in different towns.

For seven years Mary Peck Butterworth made and passed out innumerable counterfeit bills of credit without being caught. One of her passers, however, became drunk one day and boasted about the counterfeit bills in his pocket. When he was arrested, he implicated the other people involved, and the whole group was taken into custody.

When the passer became sober, he denied what he had said. He vehemently declared his innocence, maintaining that his confession had been false. The government, although it tried, could not locate any people who would testify that they had received counterfeit bills from the people arrested. Mary Peck and four of her family members were still taken to court. All the others were released.

When the case was finally presented, the finding of the court read: "The bills of presentment exhibited against Israel Peck (Mary's brother) and Mary Butterworth for forging, counterfeiting, and uttering bills of credit returned to the court by the Grand Jury with ignoramus (lacking knowledge or information) written thereupon." The case was dismissed, and Mary and her relatives went home triumphantly.

Mary continued to live in Rehoboth. She and John Butterworth had seven children, and attended church regularly. Mary died at the ripe, old age of eighty-nine. At her funeral she was eulogized as "a worthy Christian lady who had ever lived a goodly and blameless life."

Who knows, perhaps during later years Mary Peck repented of her cheating. Perhaps she began to store her treasure in heaven. We really don't know. We do know, however, that God will judge her (and all of us) according to Matthew 6:24 which says, ""No one can serve two masters; for either he will hate the one and love the other, or else he will be loyal to the one and despise the other. You cannot serve God and mammon."

Food For Thought

1. Have you ever cheated anyone? Taken a bigger share of food, of time, or of money? Have you ever taken credit for something that someone else did? How and when did you do so?
2. In the phrase "You cannot serve both God and Money," how would you describe serving money? In what way can money be a master? Is there an in-between—can you serve God a little bit and money a little bit also? Why/not?

40

In Flanders Field

"I have a letter from my uncle." Margaret Kilgour proudly waved an envelope under her friend's nose. "It's all the way from Europe— from the war front, you know." The friend eyed the envelope curiously. "What does your uncle say? Does he say anything about bullets or cannons?"

It was 1915, the time of the First World War. Many Canadians and Americans had gone overseas to fight Germany. Margaret Kilgour was Canadian. John McCrae was her uncle, and he had enlisted for service overseas in Europe. She missed him very much, but he did write letters to her and to her brothers.

"Here. I'll read you a part of Uncle John's letter." Margaret sat down on the steps in front of her house. "This is how the letter begins:"

My dear Margaret:

There is a little girl in this house whose name is Clothilde. She is ten years old and calls me Monsieur Major. How would you like it if twenty or thirty soldiers came along and lived in your house and put their horses in the shed or in the stable? There are not many little boys

> *Blessed is the man who endures temptation; for when he has been proved, he will receive the crown of life which the Lord has promised to those who love Him. James 1:12*

and girls left in this part of the country, but occasionally one meets them on the roads with baskets of eggs or loaves of bread. Most of them have no homes, for their houses have been burnt by the Germans; but they do not cry over it. It is dangerous for them, for a shell might hit them at any time, and it would not be an eggshell either."

Margaret stopped reading. Her friend was impressed.

* * * * * * *

The war was not only dangerous for children. It was also very dangerous for all the Canadian and American soldiers who were fighting against Germany. Altogether Canada had 60,000 casualties in this war.

John McCrae, Margaret's uncle, was stationed in Ypres and sitting in a dugout when he wrote the letter. Ypres is a place in northwestern Belgium. Two huge battles were fought here. A dugout was a large hole dug into the ground for soldiers to use as a shelter from bullets, and it was a dreary, unhappy place where many men died.

John McCrae was a very compassionate doctor. As a Christian he loved singing and much enjoyed going to church to hear God's Word preached. Many times if a chaplain was not readily available to help a dying man, John McCrae would speak gently to that man in the chaplain's place.

While John McCrae was in his dugout, he observed a great deal. His dressing station (or doctor's office) was at the foot of an embankment. On top of the bank men were fighting. When they were hurt, they would literally roll into his dressing station at the bottom of the bank. When the fighting stopped for a bit, there were many burials. John watched. He saw the crosses being put up on the many graves, side by side, row on row. And as the cemetery grew, flowers sprang up and larks sang in the sky above.

John worked and watched and prayed; and he was moved to write a poem. It is a poem that is often read on Remembrance Day. The poem is called "In Flanders Fields." They were the fields that John was looking at day after day. The poem reads:

> *In Flanders fields the poppies grow*
> *Between the crosses, row on row,*
> *That mark our place; and in the sky*
> *The larks, still bravely singing, fly*
> *Scarce heard amid the guns below.*
>
> *We are the Dead. Short days ago*
> *We lived, felt dawn, saw sunset glow,*
> *Loved and were loved, and now we lie,*
> *In Flanders fields.*
>
> *Take up our quarrel with the foe:*
> *To you from failing hands we throw*
> *The torch; be yours to hold it high.*
> *If ye break faith with us who die*
> *We shall not sleep, though poppies grow*
> *In Flanders fields.*

John McCrae was a Christian. When he left Canada to go overseas, he said, "I am in good hope of coming back soon and safely: that, I am glad to say, is in other and better hands than ours." He died of pneumonia in 1918 before World War I was over.

In Flanders fields the poppies grow, between the crosses, row on row, that mark our place; and in the sky the larks, still bravely singing, fly scarce heard amid the guns below.

Food For Thought

1. Most people don't know that John McCrae was first and foremost a Christian who believed that God controlled all of life. Why does his poem make you think of the very short time that we have on earth? Why is this important to think about?

2. There is a war in which all of us are presently fighting. We have a quarrel with a foe—and that foe is the devil. What is our torch?

CHRISTINE FARENHORST, author and poet, is a columnist for *Reformed Perspective* and a contributing writer for *Christian Renewal* and *God's World*. Among her books are two collections of short stories, *Suffer Annie Spence* and *The Letter Child,* and a novel, *Before My Mother's Womb*. Farenhorst has also written a collection of poems and co-authored a church history textbook for children. She and her husband, Anco, have five children and eight grandchildren.

SCOTT WILKINSON, a pastor in the Reformed Presbyterian Church, serves as a church planter in the Kitchener, Ontario, Canada, area. He and his wife, Elineke, have four children.